# H Is For ecoHome

# *eco*HOME
## An A to Z Guide To A Safer, Toxin-Free Household

A N N A  K R U G E R

AVON BOOKS  NEW YORK

## A GAIA ORIGINAL

**Conceived by** Joss Pearson

**Editorial** Libby Hoseason, Fiona Trent

**Design** Marnie Searchwell

**Illustration** Babz Scott (The Garden Studio)

**Direction** Jonathan Hilton, Patrick Nugent

Printed and bound in Italy by Rotolito s.p.a. on enviromentally friendly paper, with less than 0.5 kilos of chlorine per 100 kilos of paper.

AVON BOOKS
A division of
The Hearst Corporation,
1350 Avenue of the Americas
New York, New York 10019

Published by arrangement with Gaia Books Ltd
Library of Congress Catalog Card Number: 91-92125
ISBN: 0-380-76520-9

First Avon Books Trade Printing: February l992

AVON TRADEMARK REG. U.S. PAT. OFF.
AND IN OTHER COUNTRIES, MARCA REGISTRADA, HECHO EN U.S.A.

10 9 8 7 6 5 4 3 2 1

"Safe as Houses" is how most of us like to think of our homes. Once inside, we would expect to feel safe from the environmental problems that beset the planet and the pollution that pervades the environment. This is not necessarily the case, however. Far from our homes being safe havens, they may be significant contributors to the global problem.

With some 60,000 chemicals and innumerable synthetic materials in common, everyday use, most traditional ways of building, maintaining, furnishing, and cleaning the home have become dominated by this chemical presence. From CFCs to PCBs, formaldehyde to plasticizers, volatile solvents to phenols - all are likely to be somewhere in your home, representing a hazard to your health as well as to the planet. "Sick Building Syndrome" is the phrase used to describe the physical and mental effects of living and working in unhealthy indoor environments. Poor lighting, stale and overheated air, toxic materials, synthetic interior decoration and furnishings all place additional stress on our health and wellbeing. The "sick home" is firmly established as part of this syndrome.

So, what can you do about it? The answer is: a great deal! And the advantage you have is, since it is *your* home, you can begin today. Start in simple ways, such as changing your household cleaners or installing low-energy lights, and then move gradually up to more complex decorating and building jobs. As a priority, stop buying products that may harm you and your family as well as the planet. Avoid using nonsustainable materials, such as endangered tropical hardwoods; reduce plastics and synthetics; reuse and recycle; be economical with energy and water. On a wider level, campaign for safer products with "Green" labeling schemes declaring all product ingredients and the processes that went into their manufacture. There are many, many ways in which you can change your home and, by doing so, make the world a safer, more secure environment.

To start the ball rolling you may initially require help and guidance. So many of the concepts are new and may run counter to buying and behaviour patterns established over generations, and it can be difficult to find practical information and alternative products. How can you tell, for example, if products are harmful or not? Are safer and healthy alternatives available?

This is where *H is for ecoHome* provides an invaluable reference. It presents a wealth of well-researched, carefully compiled information, written with the consumer firmly in mind. Within its pages you will find easily accessible entries to help all of us make better, more environmentally sustainable choices for practically everything to do with the home. Whether you want to know about personal computers or paints, lighting or household cleaners, recycling or sustainable timber, *H is for ecoHome* will warn you against the hazards and, more importantly, offer you the alternatives.

So, before you do anything else at home, be guided by *H is for ecoHome*, and make your home a safer, healthier, and a happier place for you and your family.

**How to use this book**

All entries within *H is for ecoHome* are alphabetically arranged for easy reference. Rather than giving product brand names, which are not consistent between countries, or even necessarily within countries, the entries start with ingredient names, which you will find printed on the labels of an ever-increasing number of goods. Within entries, **bold** words refer you to other parts of the book where more detailed or supplementary information is to be located, as well as natural, safe alternatives. In this way, by following up the bold cross-references, you can discover as much or as little as you need to determine your purchasing decisions.

As well as product ingredients, *H is for ecoHome* also contains entries for processes and concepts, buzzwords and jargon that are increasingly used but often little understood. And interspersed throughout the book are special illustrated feature entries, which look in more detail at every room in the home. These also contain **bold** words to guide you back into the alphabetical entries wherever relevant. Finally, in the Resources listing at the back, you will find the names and addresses of useful suppliers, organizations, public bodies, and campaigning groups concerned with creating a safer, more environmentally friendly world for us all.

David Pearson, author of *The Natural House Book*

**Acetone** This colorless liquid is a common **solvent** for removing grease, stains, and nail varnish. It is an ingredient in some glues. Acetone is an irritant and the fumes can produce drowsiness if inhaled. It is also flammable. When using acetone, guard against spills and only use it in ventilated areas. See **Stain remover** for alternatives.

**Acid rain** In the US, electrical power generation creates 73 percent of acid rain. The **coal** and oil burnt in electricity-generating power stations is responsible for emissions of **sulphur dioxide**, the biggest cause of acid rain. The US emits around 21,000,000 tons of this gas each year much more than any country in Western Europe. Once it is in the atmosphere, sulphur dioxide is converted by contact with moisture into weak **sulphuric acid** that dissolves in cloud water and forms acid rain. As a result of acid rainfall, rivers and lakes are unable to support fish and other forms of aquatic life. Acid rain also encourages the leaching of toxic metals from the soil, lessens soil fertility, and kills trees. In Norway, 20 percent of lakes have no fish, while more than two-thirds of all UK forests and over half of those in Germany and Switzerland have been badly damaged by acid rain.

In 1986, the Reagan Administration formally acknowledged the need for concerted action to control acid rain. In the home, you can help to reduce the emission of acid rain by taking **energy-saving** measures.

**Acrylic** A synthetic compound and a type of **plastic**, acrylic is a versatile substance. It can be processed into a fiber for **fabrics** that are used for clothing, **carpeting**, furnishing, and blankets. Acrylic, in the form of acrylic **resins**, is also added to **paint** to make it washable and to give it flexibility and durability. It is also an ingredient of some types of **sealant**. In the US, acrylonitrile, the colorless liquid used to make acrylic resins, is a suspected carcinogen and causes breathing difficulties, headache, and nausea. See **Fabrics** and **Paint, organic** for safe alternatives.

**Acypetacs zinc** This chemical compound, based on **zinc** salts produced from a synthetic acid, is the active ingredient in some brands of **timber treatments** and masonry **paint** for home use. It acts as a **fungicide** and was developed as a substitute for the three most hazardous chemical ingredients of timber treatments: **pentachlorophenol**, **tributyltin oxide**, and **lindane**. Acypetacs zinc is an irritant to skin and eyes, and the **solvent** base in which it is dissolved emits harmful vapors, especially if there is inadequate **ventilation**. Be sure that you wear protective clothing when using products containing this substance, and guard against fire as timber treatment products are flammable. See **Timber treatments** for alternatives.

**Adhesives** A wide range of adhesives and glues is available in DIY stores for pottery, wood, leather, **cork**, **rubber**, **plastic**, etc. Many modern adhesives contain toxic **solvents** such as **toluene**. Inhaling these harmful fumes can result in intoxication, hence the dangerous practice of solvent abuse or "glue sniffing". Prolonged exposure to solvent-based adhesives can seriously damage your health, especially the vital organs and the central nervous system. Avoid solvent-based adhesives whenever possible, using water-based instead. If you must use solvent-based adhesives, make sure the space is well ventilated and keep them well away from sources of ignition, since they are also highly flammable. Solvent-based adhesives may irritate your skin.

Other types of adhesive include irritant **epoxy resins**, and "superglue" and other fast-acting adhesives containing toxic **cyanoacrylates** that can bond skin in seconds. Adhesives for wood and paper that contain **polyvinyl acetate (PVA)** are generally of low toxicity.

In response to the solvent-abuse issue, manufacturers have introduced solvent-free, water-based adhesives. Look for labels stating ingredients are "water-based" or "nontoxic". **Organic paint** suppliers also offer nontoxic adhesives based on plant-derived binders for **cork**, tiles, **linoleum**, **carpeting**, and parquet **flooring**. These adhesives are strong, elastic, and have a pleasant smell during and after application.

**Aerosols** In response to consumer pressure in the UK, leading manufacturers in the **toiletries** and, to some extent, the DIY markets, have largely phased out the **CFC** propellants used in aerosols. Today, more than 90 percent of aerosol sprays in the US are CFC-free. The alternative propellants used are usually **hydrocarbons**. These, however, can still damage the atmosphere and contribute to the **greenhouse effect**. Aerosol gases are also flammable and, because their contents are pressurized, they can explode. Keep cans away from heat sources and do not puncture them. Never throw half-empty cans away: when they are incinerated, the polluting gases are rapidly discharged into the air. The aerosol cans themselves are made up of an assortment of metals and plastics, representing a waste of both resources and energy, and they are difficult to dispose of and impossible to recycle. Opt for environmentally sound alternatives, such as the **pump-action spray**, when buying toiletries and household products.

**Aformosia** This is an endangered **tropical hardwood**. Avoid buying products made from this wood unless supplies come from managed plantations. See the list of **sustainable timber** on p. 155.

**Air cleaners** If you want to improve the quality of the air in your home, first be sure that there is plenty of natural **ventilation**. Portable filter units may also help. The air-cleaning capacity of these units ranges from a single room to a whole house. They work by drawing air through a prefilter to remove dust; main filters to absorb vapors and small gas molecules; and a filter to remove particulates, small particles of such pollutants as smoke, that remain suspended in the air. Remember to keep filters clean and change them regularly: dirty filters can turn into breeding grounds for bacteria. These filters will not remove **radon**.
Another option for improving air quality is to invest in

an **ionizer**. This will reduce levels of smoke, dust, and some allergens, as well as improving the balance between positive and negative ions. Negative ion predominance is said to be beneficial: air near running water, for example, has a high negative ion charge. A wholly natural alternative, however, is to have four or five **house plants** in rooms where air quality is poor. Plants, especially the common spider plant *Chlorophytum elatum* var. *vittatum*, are natural filters that purify indoor air by absorbing pollutants and help to regulate humidity levels.

**Air conditioning**
**Air freshener**

**Air conditioning** Some coolants in air-conditioning systems contain **CFCs** and leaking joints and seals that enable the coolant to escape into the atmosphere pose a major problem. These systems also consume large quantities of **energy**. In addition, air-conditioning systems may pose a health risk in sealed buildings where you cannot open a window. In such environments, poorly maintained air-conditioning systems may become clogged with dirt and such pollutants as **formaldehyde**. The polluted air is then recirculated and increases the spread of airborne micro-organisms and bacteria, making you more vulnerable to sickness and **sick building syndrome**. Legionnaire's disease, for example, is caused by airborne bacteria from "cooling towers" and has a 15 percent fatality rate. One recent American study into air pollution in offices found that one-third of buildings surveyed were operating entirely on continuously recycled air. The metal ducting in air-conditioning systems also attracts the beneficial negative ions, which are, therefore, prevented from circulating around the building. If you have an air-conditioning system, keep it well maintained. See also **Central heating**, **Humidifiers**, **Ionizers,** and **Ventilation**.

**Air freshener** This product does not "freshen" air, since it may contain such polluting chemicals as **naphthalene**. Aerosol varieties may also contain harmful **CFCs** or **hydrocarbons** that damage the **ozone** layer and contribute to the **greenhouse effect**. Some air fresheners work by masking odors with a stronger, synthetic odor such as **limonene**, a suspected carcinogen that has a "lemon" scent. Others coat the nasal passages with a film, or block the olfactory nerve. Such chemical-based air fresheners impair your sense of smell and this may effectively prevent you from smelling stale food, or even if something is burning. Some people are allergic to the chemicals and synthetic perfumes in air fresheners, and develop symptoms including respiratory problems and headaches. Avoid synthetic air fresheners and freshen your air naturally with scented **house plants**, **herbs**, and flowers, and open a window to disperse odors. You can also sweeten the air by placing bowls of **pot-pourri** around the house, or use your favorite **essential oils** in incensors or vaporizers. To deodorize the inside of the **refrigerator**, leave an opened packet of **baking powder** inside.

**Alcohol** See **Ethanol, Isopropanol, Methanol**.

**Aldehydes** This group of **organic** chemicals is based on carbon, hydrogen, and oxygen. Aldehydes have strong odors. A common aldehyde found in the home is **formaldehyde**.

**Aluminum** This light, malleable metal has many uses, including **cookware**, **cooking foil**, and **drink cans**. It is also found in food and **drinking water**. In large quantities aluminum poses clear health problems: high intake is thought to be linked to Alzheimer's disease, or premature senility. Aluminum is present in most beverages, particularly tea, and cereals, and it can leach from pans and foil into acidic foods, such as tomatoes. To reduce your aluminum intake avoid cooking with it and using aluminum tea pots. Instead of foil, cook with and wrap food in greaseproof paper, and use stainless-steel, cast-iron, or glass cookware. **Acid rain** also encourages the leaching of aluminum from the soil into rivers and the water supply.

Aluminum is expensive, and processing it requires vast amounts of **energy**. The metal is extracted from bauxite, some of which is found in rainforest areas. Since this results in the destruction of vast areas of forest, the extraction process is a cause for environmental concern. Bauxite then has to be cleaned with **caustic soda**, which, once discharged into rivers, also pollutes water supplies. If you are buying new doors and window frames, choose **wooden** instead of aluminum frames. Empty aluminum cans are ideal for **recycling**. It takes 95 percent less energy to make a can from recycled aluminum than it does to make one from the raw metal. Some local charities collect aluminum

11

foil bottle tops. You can also save these, as well as used aluminum for cleaning silver. See **Metal polish**.

**Aluminum chlorohydrate** This **aluminum** salt is commonly found in **antiperspirants** and some **deodorants**. It works by blocking pores and preventing perspiration. Since this chemical irritates the skin, it should not be used on cracked or sore areas. It can also harm your eyes. In view of the potentially harmful effects of aluminum described above, do not use products containing aluminum chloro-hydrate regularly. See **Deodorant** for safe alternatives.

**Ammonia** This colorless, pungent gas is commonly found, in solution, in household cleaners. At room temperature these products can **outgas** ammonia fumes. Ammonia is a strong irritant to eyes and the respiratory system. It can also cause burns if splashed on your skin. Never mix ammonia-based cleaning products with **chlorine bleach**: this releases toxic chlorine gas. See also **Bleach**, **Scouring powder**, **Window cleaner**.

**Aluminum chlorohydrate**
**Ammonia**
**Ammonium oxalate**
**Amyl acetate**
**Animal testing**

**Ammonium oxalate** This **ammonia** compound is found in some **metal polishes**, especially chrome polish. It is highly toxic and a powerful irritant. Guard against splashes on your skin or in your eyes. Oxalates – oxalic acid salts – are strongly corrosive substances and, if swallowed, can severely damage the kidneys. Keep well out of the reach of children. See **Metal polish** for alternatives.

**Amyl acetate** This colorless liquid with the odor of pear drops, is found in lacquers and nail varnishes. Amyl acetate is a **solvent**, and is harmful if swallowed or inhaled. Prolonged exposure to the fumes given off irritates the eyes, nose, and throat, and can cause drowsiness. Amyl acetate is flammable: only use this substance in well-ventilated areas and guard against fire.

**Animal testing** It has been estimated that, worldwide, the cosmetics and toiletries industry each year uses more than 200,000 animals – usually rabbits, guinea pigs, rats, and mice – to test their products. The Draize test, for example, involves dripping shampoo into rabbits' eyes. Face and skin creams are tested on the shaved and scratched skin of guinea pigs or rabbits, while in the Lethal Dose 50 percent

(LD50) test, rats, and guinea pigs are force fed huge amounts of products such as toothpaste or lipstick until 50 percent of them are poisoned to death.

One recent poll commissioned by the British Union for the Abolition of Vivisection (BUAV), found that 85 percent of people questioned were against cosmetic and toiletry tests on animals. Choose from the increasingly wide range of **cruelty-free** toiletries and cosmetics that are guaranteed not to have been tested on animals.

**Antifreeze** This commonly contains **propylene glycol** or **ethylene glycol**. These are toxic **solvents** that can irritate your skin and eyes. Keep antifreeze well away from children and guard against spills. Do not pour antifreeze down the drain. See **Hazardous waste** for disposal.

**Antiperspirant** A common active ingredient of antiperspirants and some **deodorants** is **aluminum chlorohydrate**, a skin irritant that is also harmful to your eyes. Aerosol varieties may contain **CFCs**. See also **Deodorant**.

**Ant killer Pesticides** that kill ants may contain hazardous chemicals. Proprietary ant killers that contain **chlordane**, **dichlorvos**, or **lindane**, should certainly be avoided. Less toxic pesticides are **pyrethrum** and **tetramethrin**. A safer alternative is **borax**: mix with equal parts of sugar and leave it where the ants are getting in, but make sure children and pets do not eat it. For a simple and natural ant deterrent, sprinkle dried chilli or dried paprika around doors and baseboards. Planting mint outside the house also helps to deter ants.

**Aphid killer** Aphids, or greenfly, can attack house as well as garden plants. Avoid powerful insecticides containing **chlordane**, **dichlorvos**, or **lindane**. **Pyrethrum** is a less toxic alternative but the safest option is to spray the plant with soft soap. This soap, not to be confused with household soap, is a mixture of vegetable oils and potash. It is available from garden suppliers and will not harm plants. Spray them liberally for three or four days.

**Aquabase paint** This term describes **paint**, such as emulsion or distemper, that is water- rather than oil-based.

13

**Aromatic compounds** These are **organic** chemical compounds, commonly used as **solvents**. The simplest example is **benzene**. The term also refers to compounds, such as **toluene**, that have similar properties to benzene. Aromatic compounds are flammable and harmful substances. Benzene, for example, is carcinogenic.

**Arsenic compounds** These highly toxic compounds are commonly used as **pesticides** and **fungicides** to treat **timber** while it is still in plank form. Treated timber is most hazardous in the first two weeks after treatment and contact at this stage can result in arsenic poisoning. The lethal dose for adults is only half a gram of arsenic. Touching treated timber without protective gloves may result in such skin problems as dermatitis, loss of skin pigment, and even skin cancer. Arsenic compounds can cause cancer of the liver and, according to data from the US Environmental Protection Agency, they are responsible for abnormal development of the fetus.

**Artificial lighting** It has been estimated that in the more affluent countries, 80 to 90 percent of our lives is spent indoors, without the benefit of daylight. Natural light is essential for good health and is a primary stimulus for the skin to manufacture vitamin D – essential for good teeth and bones. Many homes and workplaces have a poor supply of natural light and, in winter months, we may rely too heavily on artificial light: the common forms supply little ultraviolet light. Some people can be sensitive to reduced supplies of daylight and suffer from Seasonal Affective Disorder or SAD Syndrome; symptoms include depression, lethargy, craving for carbohydrates, and weight gain. Use light colors in your home to reflect daylight, paint outside walls white, and use light-colored paving. Consider, also, installing some **full-spectrum lighting**, which has a similar color spectrum to daylight.

Artificial lighting may not be **energy efficient** while older **fluorescent lights** may contain harmful **PCBs**. See **Light bulbs** for energy-saving and healthier alternatives.

**Asbestos** This group of fibrous minerals has a high resistance to heat. Uses of asbestos once included fireproofing and **insulation material** in buildings, brake and clutch linings, and **paint**. Although asbestos-based building supplies are being phased out, asbestos-based **cement** boarding for walls, asbestos piping and corrugated roofing may, however, still be available from some building suppliers and should be avoided. Asbestos comes in three types, blue, brown, or white, and they are all dangerous. The fibers are sharp and durable and can remain embedded in body tissue. Exposure to airborne asbestos fiber can result in the serious lung disease asbestosis, and to lung cancer to which smokers with reduced lung function are particularly vulnerable. Although the use of asbestos is now being strictly limited, it is still present in older houses in the form of fireproofing; in insulation material around pipes, **boilers**, tanks; in roof and floor tiles; and in **boards**. Old **ovens** may contain asbestos in their walls or door seals. Wear and tear on protective coverings, or on joints and seals, may expose asbestos-containing material. This allows asbestos fibers to float freely in the air and some can remain airborne for up to 20 hours.

**Ash, European**
**Ash, White**
**Aspen**

If you have, or suspect you may have, asbestos in your home, especially any that is crumbling or flaking, *DO NOT try to remove it yourself. Seek expert advice from your local health department immediately.*

**Ash, European** A **hardwood** grown in the UK and Europe, ash is a **sustainable timber**. See the list of sustainable timber on p. 155.

**Ash, White** This **hardwood** is grown in North America and is a **sustainable timber**. See the list of sustainable timber on p. 155.

**Aspen** This **hardwood** grows in the UK, Europe, and North America and is included in the list of **sustainable timber** on p. 155.

Food preparation and storage require hygienic conditions but the materials we use in our kitchens can result in both a poor-quality environment and denatured food. The modern kitchen is also wasteful of both **energy** and other resources, especially **water**.

**Stoves** Gas stoves use less energy than electric models, and **gas** production causes less environmental pollution. However, gas stoves cause indoor pollution. To minimize this and **condensation**, install an **extractor fan**, open windows, or fit a **stove hood**.

**Refrigerator, freezer** A well-stocked refrigerator is more **energy-efficient** than a half-empty one, but overfilled shelves will not allow the air to circulate. To save energy, site your refrigerator well away from the stove and defrost it regularly. The coolants used in refrigerators contain **CFCs** that deplete the **ozone** layer. If you are buying a refrigerator, choose a low CFC, energy-efficient model.

**Washing machine, dishwasher** These machines use a great deal of energy and water. Wait until you have enough clothes or dishes for a full load – full loads use proportionately less energy, especially when combined with an economy setting. Avoid machines that are cold-fill only, since heating water in them is expensive. Use **biodegradable**, **phosphate**-free **laundry powders**.

**Microwave** A UK government survey found that a third of microwave ovens tested did not heat food thoroughly. A safer way to cook food rapidly is with a **pressure cooker**. Stir-frying in a wok is another fast cooking method.

**Kitchen units** Many units made from such products as **chip-board** give off harmful **formaldehyde** vapor. **Solvent**-based **adhesives** used for laminated **plastic** worktops can also emit vapor. Choose units made from a solid **softwood** or low-emission board. For worktops, ceramic or quarry tiles, sealed **cork**, and **wood** are healthy alternatives, and a marble slab is excellent for pastry making.

**Cooking utensils** Avoid **aluminum** pans, since this metal can migrate into food. **Nonstick** pans, coated with plastic, may give off harmful fumes when hot, while older, enameled cookware may contain toxic **cadmium**. For cooking, choose stainless-steel, cast-iron, or new enameled pans.

**Household cleaners Bleach** and **scouring powder** contain chemical irritants. Choose nontoxic **biodegradable** cleaners, or such safe basics as **borax**, **bicarbonate of soda**, lemon juice, **vinegar**, and **washing soda**.

**Packaging** Some varieties of **clingfilm** contain **PVC** plasticizers that can migrate into food. Choose clingfilm that is labeled PVC or plasticizer-free, or use a biodegradable wrapping such as greaseproof **paper** or **cellophane**. **Plastic** containers can also **outgas**, so store food in glass, ceramic, or stainless-steel containers.

**Waste** To reduce waste avoid buying overpackaged products. Sort your waste into categories, such as metal, cans, glass, paper, and plastics, for **recycling** and add waste food to the compost heap.

**Water** Much of our drinking water is contaminated with **chlorine**, metals, **nitrates**, and **pesticides**. Use a jug-type **water filter** to reduce chemical and metal residues, or fit a full in-line filtering system.

**Kitchen**

**Baby-care products** A baby's skin is extremely sensitive,
and so **toiletries** for babies are likely to be less harsh than
comparable adult products. Even so, synthetic perfumes
and chemicals in such baby-care products as, for example,
talcum powder may cause skin and respiratory irritations.
Soaps and powders made from natural ingredients, often
plant-based, provide a gentle, safe alternative to synthetic
products. Calendula powder is soothing and alleviates
skin rashes; or you can buy baby powder based on
cornflour. The manufacture of baby-care products is
almost certain to involve **animal testing**. If you object to
products tested on animals, choose **cruelty-free** baby products instead.

The environmental issue of greatest concern to the
whole baby-care industry is that of disposable **diapers**.
The industrial, **chlorine** bleaching of the wood pulp that
makes up the padding of diapers, may cause **dioxin** contamination. Dioxins are suspected carcinogens. The problems associated with the disposal of diapers have also
given cause for alarm, from both a personal health and an
environmental health perspective. See **Diapers** for safe
alternatives. Cotton wool and cotton buds may also have
been treated with **chlorine bleach**. Check labels carefully
and choose unbleached varieties, or brands that are
bleached with **hydrogen peroxide**.

**Baking soda, Baking powder** See **Bicarbonate of soda**.

**Ballast** Known also as rapid-start ballasts, these are the starting devices for **fluorescent lights**. Ballasts manufactured before 1978 are likely to contain **polychlorinated biphenyls (PCBs)**. These highly toxic substances, used because they made excellent electrical insulators, are suspected carcinogens. PCBs may be released from older fluorescents, especially if the ballast is defective. Carefully replace the entire light and treat as **hazardous waste**. See **Lighting** for alternatives.

**Bamboo** This fast-growing, light but exceptionally strong cane has a multitude of uses, from scaffolding to furniture, and is a versatile and sturdy material for your home. Bamboo gives rooms an attractive, natural look, and is a less expensive material for home furnishing than **wood**. All bamboo is imported and will probably have been treated with **pesticides** in its country of origin Avoid items with canes that have dark flecks: they are almost certain to have been treated. You can, however, seal in any toxic coating by giving bamboo a protective finish with natural **varnish** or **shellac**.

**Bat-friendly treatments** If bats are roosting in your attic, you can get a local conservation group to move them. Bats, however, are harmless and it is illegal in Britain to harm or kill them. If you plan to use **timber treatments** in the roof space, seek advice from a conservation group and choose a brand that will not harm the bats. Check labels carefully and choose treatments based on such bat-friendly chemicals as **permethrin**. This substance is is not toxic to bats and is considered to be a safer option for people. See also **Timber treatments**.

**Bath** A standard tub can take up to 36 gallons of hot water as opposed to the 18 gallons used during a five-minute shower, and water is expensive to heat. Showering instead of bathing, therefore, costs less in terms of natural resources and **energy**. Enamel baths retain heat more efficiently than plastic or fiberglass types.

**Batteries** There are four main types of battery commonly available: low-power **zinc** chloride or zinc carbon batteries for clocks and **calculators**; alkaline batteries used in cameras and personal stereos; nickel-cadmium rechargeable batteries that can be reused up to a thousand times; and small, high-power button cell batteries used in watches and hearing aids. Zinc chloride, alkaline, rechargeable, and button cell batteries can contain **mercury** and **cadmium**, both toxic metals. These metals are not **biodegradable** and once deposited in landfills with the rest of the household rubbish, they can leach out and contaminate water supplies. Fish, for example, will absorb mercury and then pass it on through the food chain. In Japan, batteries are classified as toxic waste and deposited at service stations for safe disposal.

Some manufacturers in the US, UK, and Europe have begun reducing levels of mercury and cadmium from batteries in favor of alternative ingredients. Cadmium, however, is an essential part of the recharging mechanism, so it cannot be removed although it can be recycled.
European Community (EC) legislation sets maximum, and very low, levels for these metals and encourages recycling programs. Many manufacturers throughout Europe collect rechargeables for recycling.

Batteries are not energy-efficient: manufacturing them uses 50 times more energy than they will ever produce. Avoiding battery-powered appliances and choosing equipment that runs on household power is the most **energy saving** option. If this is not practicable, opt for rechargeable batteries and use a solar-powered recharger.

**Bed**

**Bed** Traditional beds tend to have **metal** frames and bedsprings, and many mattresses are also sprung. Research from Europe and America suggests that metal, a good conductor of electricity, becomes magnetized via domestic wiring and electrical appliances in the **bedroom** (p. 112). According to specialists, this can result in exposure to increased radiation from **electromagnetic fields (EMFs)** of increasing strength, which can then interfere with the electrical impulses of our bodies. Symptoms associated with increased exposure to EMFs are known collectively as electrostress, and include sickness, headache, nausea, sweating, and insomnia. To reduce your exposure to electrostress, choose a non-conducting wooden bed, and a mattress without metal springs, or with non-magnetic springs. You can also fit a **neutralizing undersheet** that, it is claimed, offers protection against EMFs. See also **Electromagnetic fields**, and **Neutralizing undersheet**.

A bed with a solid wood frame and a natural fiber-filled mattress or **futon** is the healthiest option. A sturdy, slatted **wood** base with a firm mattress made from natural fibers will provide the support your body needs. Slatted wood allows air to circulate through the mattress. Mattresses or futons made from such materials as **cotton** and **wool**, breathe, absorb, and release moisture. If you are asthmatic or suffer from other allergies, **latex** foam mattresses are ideal. Avoid mattresses and pillows made from **polyurethane foam**. Should the foam catch fire, it would release suffocating, toxic fumes. Mattresses and futon covers may have been treated with a **fire retardant**, a process involving **formaldehyde**. Cover them with a natural wool blanket or fleece: see **Bedding**. If you are buying a new wooden bed, make sure that the lumber used is from a **sustainable** source, and not a **tropical hardwood**. **Softwoods**, such as **pine**, make excellent bed bases and can be finished with a nontoxic **varnish** or **beeswax**.

**Bedding**

**Bedding** Many sheets, pillowcases, and **duvet** or comforter covers are made from synthetic fibers, such as **polyester**, or a mixture of a natural fiber, **cotton**, and polyester, to make **"poly-cotton blends"**. Blankets may contain synthetic **acrylic** fiber. Polyester/cotton mixtures have been treated with **formaldehyde**, a suspected carcinogen. This same chemical is used to treat fabrics to reduce creasing, and is present in bed linen labeled **"easy care"**, **"permanent press"**, or **"non-iron"**. Treated fabric, however, is not always labeled, and it is impossible to tell if a finish has been applied. Formaldehyde binds to the fabric and may remain on it permanently. As a precaution, soak all new bed linen and wash it thoroughly in hot water before use.

Cotton used for bedding will almost certainly have been treated with **pesticides** during growth, and then whitened with **bleach** before dyeing. Soak and hot wash to reduce pesticide residues, or choose **organic**, unbleached, cotton bed linen from specialist suppliers. Cotton flannel is another alternative; it is warm and needs no ironing. Choose duvets filled with pure down, rather than polyester, and light, cellular wool blankets, which are warmer and healthier than acrylic mixtures. Another natural, and luxurious, way to keep warm is a tufted lambs' wool underblanket. This is also a safer option than an **electric blanket**.

**Beech, American** This temperate **hardwood** is native to North America, and is a **sustainable timber**. See the list of sustainable timber on p. 155.

**Beeswax** Bees secrete this wax and use it to construct their cells. It is a wholly natural product and is commonly used as a quality **furniture polish**. Beeswax will nourish, restore, and preserve **wood** furniture that has not been **varnished**, such as stripped **pine**, and antique items. It gives a durable and protective finish, as well as a deep shine, and is much healthier for you and your furniture than the type of **aerosol**, **silicone** spray polish which usually contains harmful **solvents**. Good quality beeswax polishes are a combination of beeswax, **turpentine** and **linseed oil**, with nothing else added. Avoid brands with added solvents such as **toluene**. You can also make your own polish – see **Polish, floor and furniture**.

**Benzalkonium chloride** This **quaternary ammonium compound** is a **fungicide** commonly found in some cleaning products and **wood preservatives**. It irritates the skin and eyes and is poisonous if swallowed.

**Benzene** An **aromatic compound** which occurs naturally in crude oil, and is also found in **gasoline** and **petroleum** mixtures. It may also be added to gasoline, particularly unleaded gasoline to raise the octane level and improve performance. Although in its pure form benzene is not commonly found in DIY products, it may be combined with other **solvents** in some **paint strippers**. It is a highly toxic chemical which in high doses is carcinogenic, attacking the blood system and causing leukemia. In Los Angeles, smog contaminated with benzene is responsible for an estimated extra 220 cases of cancer each year. Repeated inhalation of low doses can result in symptoms ranging from headaches and dizziness to bleeding gums. It is also a potent skin irritant. According to the US Environmental Protection Agency, there is no safe level of benzene.

Most benzene in the atmosphere is emitted by car exhausts. Air pollution surveys carried out in 1989 found atmospheric benzene levels in UK cities were two to three times higher than in California. Greater exposure to this chemical, however, is most likely to occur at filling stations. Benzene is responsible for the distinctive smell of gasoline: it evaporates from the pump nozzle when you fill up your car. In California, filling stations are required to display notices warning of the risks of inhaling benzene, while special extractor pumps can prevent benzene vapors from escaping into the atmosphere. Where legislation to limit benzene emissions does not yet exist, protect yourself by standing back from your car while filling up.

**Benzoyl peroxide** The curing agent in two-part wood **filler**, benzoyl peroxide is an irritant and also highly flammable. Keep any filler containing this compound away from your eyes and off your skin. Ensure also that it is well clear of any sources of ignition. A safer alternative is an oil-based filler paste available from **organic paint** suppliers.

**Benzoyl peroxide**
**Bicarbonate of soda**
**Biodegradable**

**Bicarbonate of soda** Known also as **baking soda** or, in modified form, **baking powder**, bicarbonate of soda is the common name of sodium bicarbonate, a white crystalline solid, often used in powdered form as a raising agent in baking. Bicarbonate of soda makes an excellent nontoxic, general-purpose household cleaner: sprinkle it on a damp cloth and use it as an alternative to **scouring powder**. It will clean sinks, tiles, working surfaces, and baths, and is easily rinsed off. For an effective **carpet cleaner**, shake it on your carpets and rugs, then vacuum off after an hour or two. Mixed with **vinegar**, bicarbonate of soda makes a good **drain cleaner**. You can also make a paste with water and spread it on a cool **oven** to soften baked-on spills. And if your clothes have perspiration stains, soak them in water with a handful of bicarbonate of soda.

Bicarbonate of soda is a versatile product around the home. You can deodorize the inside of your refrigerator by leaving an opened packet inside. Bicarbonate of soda is also a safe, effective, alternative to commercial **antiperspirant**, and makes a good tooth-cleaning powder if you run out of **toothpaste**.

**Biodegradable** Products that are biodegradable are easily assimilated into the environment, since they disintegrate without causing pollution. The ingredients can be broken down naturally into organic matter and minerals by the action of the microorganisms present in water, soil, and air. Currently, this term is applied to a range of products, including **laundry powder**, **dishwashing liquid**, **household cleaners**, and **shampoo**. The term also applies to materials used as **packaging** for products. For a product to be completely biodegradable, both ingredients and packaging materials should decompose without polluting.

**Biological** This broad term is used to describe **laundry powders** containing **enzymes** – substances that digest protein and starch stains, such as blood or chocolate, from clothing. Biological does *not* mean natural, neither does it mean that the product is environmentally harmless or **biodegradable**. On the contrary, enzymes have been linked with such allergic reactions as skin rashes and respiratory problems. See **Laundry powder** for safe alternatives.

**Birch, Yellow** This is a **hardwood** grown in North America and may be used in general joinery, woodenware, and furniture. Birch is a **sustainable timber** that is also grown in the UK and Europe. See the list on p. 155 for other sustainable timbers.

**Bisphenol A-epichlorohydrin** An active ingredient of **adhesives** based on **epoxy resin**, such adhesive is described on product labels as a "reaction product". Epoxy resins are powerful irritants and the vapor they give off is toxic. Only use these products in well-ventilated conditions and do not spill on your skin. See **Adhesives** for alternatives.

**Bitumen** A black, tar-like, mineral residue derived from **petroleum**, bitumen is waterproof. Widely used as a **roofing material**, as a **sealant**, and as a protective covering for wall and ceiling **boards**, bitumen is also an ingredient of exterior **paint** for roofs and guttering. It is both a skin irritant, and poisonous if swallowed. Wear gloves when using it and ensure that you do not spill any on your skin. It is also flammable so keep it away from open flames.

**Bleach** Household bleach is a harsh chemical product bought for use as **toilet**, **sink**, and **drain**, and **laundry cleaner**. Bleaches come in two types: the first is based on **sodium hypochlorite** and is known as **chlorine bleach**; the second is based on **hydrogen peroxide** and is known as **oxygen bleach**. The active chemicals in bleach give off irritating fumes and can burn your skin. Strong chlorine bleach is also a **water** pollutant. It is toxic to fish and other forms of aquatic life, and kills the beneficial bacteria that break down sewage in septic tanks. It can also release toxic chlorine gas if mixed with other toilet-bowl cleaners. The chlorine bleaching process of **paper** products, from **toilet paper** to disposable **diapers**, produces highly toxic **dioxins**, suspected carcinogens and environmental contaminants. Oxygen bleach is a less aggressive substance for the home as well as for the environment, but it is still irritating to your eyes and skin, and harmful if swallowed. Always use bleach very sparingly and avoid concentrated bleach. Try nontoxic alternatives based on such natural ingredients as **vinegar**. See individual active ingredients of bleach and for safer alternatives see **Toilet cleaner**, **Scouring powder**, **Drain cleaner**, **Laundry powder**.

**Blockboard** This laminated **board** is a type of **plywood**. The inner core is built up from pieces of solid **wood** blocks, laid side by side. Like the other boards, blockboard is bonded with **formaldehyde** in the form of **urea formaldehyde** resin which, once in the home, can **outgas**. Blockboard is now used only rarely for furniture.

Blockboard
Blue Angel
Board

**Blue Angel** This symbol is found on a range of some 3000 German products and is understood by 80 percent of the shoppers in that country. The Blue Angel is an officially approved label, displayed on products that have met certain environmental standards. It was introduced by the German government in 1978, making it the longest-running of the environmental labelling programs currently in operation anywhere in the world. The product criteria that must be fulfilled in order to display the symbol range from **packaging** suitable for **recycling**, to ingredients that are not wasteful of natural resources, for example, recycled **paper**. But the symbol may also be displayed in cases where the harmful ingredient of a product has been reduced, but not eliminated. Although recognized as the official environmental label, the Blue Angel program is, however, voluntary, and this does not prevent manufacturers from using their own unofficial labels.

**Board** There are three main categories of board: laminated board, **compositeboard**, and **fiberboard**. In the home, the most common laminated board is **plywood**, and previously

**blockboard**; the most commonly used compositeboard is **chipboard**; and the best known of the fiberboards are **hardboard** and **medium density fiberboard (MDF)**. In the home, boards have many and varied uses, from flooring, roofing, and furniture to shelving. One of their main advantages is that they are less expensive than solid **wood**. Their main disadvantage, however, is that the manufacturing process of all these types of board uses synthetic **formaldehyde** resin, or **adhesives** containing formaldehyde, to bond together the components of the board. Formaldehyde is a suspected carcinogen. Always seal board products with nontoxic **paint** or **varnish**. Choose products made from a **sustainable timber**. For **flooring**, chipboard bonded with cement rather than formaldehyde is available from specialist suppliers.

**Boiler** An **energy-efficient** hydronic boiler heating system can save energy consumption in the home, but for maximum effect it must be combined with such additional methods as increased **insulation**. A **gas-condensing boiler** is the most fuel efficient of boilers currently available. Burning **gas** is more cost efficient than electricity. Molecule for molecule, it produces about 40 percent less **carbon dioxide** when burnt than coal and causes less environmental pollution. Conventional boilers are around 70 percent efficient; the rest of the heat escapes through the flue. The gas-condensing boiler extracts the heat from the flue gases, achieving up to 20 percent greater efficiency than other gas boilers, and resulting in a significant saving on fuel bills. See also **Furnace**.

**Borax** Sodium tetraborate, or borax, is a naturally occurring mineral salt, available from any chemist in the form of a purified, fine, white powder. Borax has cleaning, disinfecting, bleaching, and deodorizing properties. When tested at an American hospital, borax was found to satisfy their requirements for a good disinfectant. It is a most versatile alternative household product: you can use it safely instead of chemical-based **bleach**, **scouring powder**, **disinfectant**, and **stain remover**. Borax also dispels odors from garbage bins. As a household cleaner, apply it with a damp cloth, or dissolved in water; it rinses off easily. Plain soap mixed with borax also makes a gentle cleaner for fabrics that need to be washed by hand.

The other principal use of borax is as an **insecticide** and **fungicide**. Sprinkle borax in damp areas, such as **basements** (p. 50), where **mold** or mildew might form. It also makes an effective **ant killer**, mixed with sugar. Borax is an alternative to toxic **wood preservative**: impregnating wood with borax solution will protect it against fungus and woodworm. Borax wood treatments are available in commercially-manufactured form, or you can buy powdered borax and treat small areas of wood or items of furniture yourself.

Borax in contact with unbroken skin does not present a problem, but it is wise to wear gloves if you have particularly sensitive skin. If swallowed, however, borax is toxic so keep it well away from children and pets.

Boron compounds
Bottles

**Boron compounds** These chemical compounds, which belong to the same group as **borax**, are commonly employed as **fungicides** and **insecticides**. Produced in the form of liquid, powder, and water-soluble rods and pellets, boron is prepared as a soaking bath or inserted into drilled holes to stop wet rot. It is suitable for window frames and exterior woodwork. According to the Environmental Protection Agency, boron is one of the few acceptable chemical **timber treatments** available, and it is **bat-friendly**. Keep the rods well out of the reach of children, since they may be tempted to chew them.

**Bottles** Americans discard nearly 2.5 million **plastic** drink bottles as **waste** every 60 minutes. Although certain types of plastic are suitable for **recycling**, many facilities, where they exist at all, are minimal. **Glass** bottles, on the other hand, can be successfully recycled, and most local municipalities provide a **bottle bank** or reclamation center for recycling. Choosing bottles made from glass, rather than plastic, and disposing of them in your local bottle bank after use is the most environmentally sound option. You can also buy returnable deposit bottles. In France, beer is sold in standard bottles that can be returned to any supermarket to be cleaned and refilled. In the UK, the returnable milk bottle is reused around 24 times. This wastes fewer natural resources and the glass bottles are also healthier than waxed **paper** and plastic cartons since toxic **dioxins** from **chlorine-bleached** milk cartons can leach into your milk. See also **Recycling**.

**Bottle banks** In the UK and Europe, jars and **bottles** made of **glass** can be deposited in bottle banks. The glass is then recycled and can be reused over and over again, with no appreciable reduction in quality, saving raw materials and energy. In 1985 Austria had one bank for every 1200 people, and the Netherlands, one for every 1400. 1990 statistics show that the UK had only one bottle bank per 12,000 people and by 1991, the UK target will be one bottle bank per 10,000, still way below European and US standards. See also **Recycling**.

**Bottled gas heater** These portable heaters run on **liquefied petroleum gas (LPG)**, either **butane** or **propane**. Both types of gas may cause drowsiness in confined spaces, since they use up oxygen and give off **carbon dioxide**. Bottled gas heaters also produce **condensation**, which may lead to **moisture** problems. Store cylinders carefully as the gas is highly flammable, and have your heater serviced regularly to prevent leaks. Be certain that rooms with this type of heating are well ventilated.

**Bottle banks**
**Bottled gas heater**
**Bottled water**

**Bottled water** Much of the **drinking water** in the US does not meet the Federal Safe Drinking Water Act of 1974 standards, and many people find that it tastes unpleasant. In response to the demand for healthier, palatable water, sales of bottled, or **mineral water** have flourished. Bottled water, however, is expensive: it costs more than 600 times as much as metered tap water and it may not be any purer or healthier. Surveys have shown that the mineral content of bottled water is not, on average, high enough to make any significant contribution to your overall health. On the contrary, in February 1990, stocks of "Perrier" water were withdrawn from sale when supplies were accidentally contaminated with carcinogenic **benzene**. Barring accidents, mineral water does, however, contain appreciably lower levels of such common tap-water pollutants as **lead** or **aluminum**. But one disadvantage of bottled water is the level of bacteria, with still water containing much higher levels than carbonated varieties. While these levels of bacteria are not harmful to adults, it is always advisable to boil still mineral water that is intended for babies. Buy mineral water in **glass**, not **plastic** bottles, whenever possible. See also **Water filters**.

**Brake and clutch fluid** The range of chemicals used in these products may irritate sensitive skin. Take used or left over fluid to a reclamation center for **recycling**, or to a service station offering this facility.

**Brass polish** See **Metal polish** for active ingredients and safe alternatives.

**Bromadiolone** This chemical is a powerful **rat and mouse poison** so keep it well away from children and pets. Bromadiolone is also harmful to birds of prey if they eat poisoned rodents. See also **Rat and mouse poison**.

**Butane** This flammable **liquefied petroleum gas** is used as a heating fuel in portable **bottled gas heaters**. Butane, a **hydrocarbon** gas, is also used in **propane torches**, camping stoves, cigarette lighters, and as a substitute propellant for **CFCs** in **aerosols**. See **Bottled gas heater**.

**Butanol** This colorless, volatile, flammable liquid is widely employed as a **solvent**. The vapors given off by butanol can cause headaches and dizziness. It is also a skin and eye irritant, and may cause dermatitis. Only use solvents containing butanol in areas with plenty of ventilation, and guard against spilling it on your skin.

**Cadmium** This is a heavy metal found in **batteries**, and in pigments to color industrial **paint**, glazes for pottery, and **plastic**. In the home, plastic dishwashing bowls and buckets that are bright red, orange, or yellow in color may contain cadmium. It is also found in older kinds of orange- or red-enameled **cookware**. Cadmium and its compounds are extremely toxic in low concentrations: repeated small doses can damage the heart, kidneys, and liver. Even small quantities of cadmium in children can cause bone anomalies, and there is some evidence that continued exposure to low levels reduces the growth rate of unborn babies. EC legislation is expected to limit allowable levels of cadmium used by industry to an absolute minimum. In some European countries, for example, Sweden and Switzerland, batteries containing cadmium must be labeled as environmentally hazardous.

To avoid cadmium in your home, choose plastic houseware that is labeled "cadmium-free". Increasing numbers of cadmium-free batteries are also on sale.

**Calcium hypochlorite** A chemical compound containing **chlorine**, calcium hypochlorite is the active ingredient of **scouring powder** based on **bleach**. Calcium hypochlorite irritates the skin and eyes, and is highly toxic by inhalation. When using bleaching powder, wear gloves to protect your skin, and do not breathe in the dust. See **Scouring powder** for safe alternatives.

**Calcium plumbate** This compound contains **lead** and is found in **primer** for painting such exterior metalwork as window frames. It is a suspected carcinogen. Avoid products containing this compound and choose from the lead-free primers available. See also **Paint, organic**.

**Calculator** For the **home office** (p. 176) choose solar-powered calculators that use only renewable solar energy. Since they do not need **batteries**, they work out cheaper, and create less **waste**.

**Candles** Most commercial brands of candles are made from animal fat or **paraffin** wax. If you prefer to avoid these substances, choose candles made from **beeswax**.

**Cans** In the US, over 70 billion cans are used each year. Cans are composed mainly of tin-plate and steel, or **aluminum**. Tin cans used for food may present a health risk if a **lead** compound is used to solder the seam of the can. Some food manufacturers have removed the need for solder by changing to tin-free steel that can be welded. Some products may also be packaged in cans with an inert white lining that is electronically sealed.

Extracting the ore and the manufacture of cans uses vast amounts of **energy**. Both these stages are environmentally polluting, and consume large quantities of valuable natural resources. Over four tons of bauxite, for example, are needed to make one ton of aluminum. Metals are not **biodegradable** and since they account for about ten percent by weight of US domestic refuse, they generate an immense amount of **waste**.

The metal component of all cans, however, can be reused. This conserves both energy and raw materials, which directly benefits the environment. The US recycles 65 percent of its cans each year, Australia 50 percent, Japan 45 percent, and the UK 2 percent. See **Recycling** for information on can disposal.

**Carbaryl** This insecticide is commonly used in flea preparations for household pets. Banned in Germany, carbaryl has caused mutations in cells of laboratory animals. It is highly toxic and can be absorbed through your skin. See **Flea powder** for safer alternatives.

**Carbon dioxide (CO$_2$)** Of the four main greenhouse gases, CO$_2$ is the major warming gas, accounting for about 50 percent of the total **greenhouse effect**. In 1860 the CO$_2$ content of the atmosphere was about 280 parts per million (ppm) by volume; today this figure has increased to 350ppm, and by the year 2040 the figure is estimated to be at least 500ppm.

The rise of CO$_2$ is due mainly to the burning of **fossil fuels** – **coal** and **gas** by industry, and oil (in the form of **gasoline**) in the internal-combustion engine. Each car, for example, produces four times its own weight in CO$_2$ every year. At present the only way to reduce levels of CO$_2$ significantly is to consume less **energy**. The US is responsible for adding 1.5 billion tons of CO$_2$ to the atmosphere each year. Planners at the UK Department of Energy expect a 73 percent increase in their CO$_2$ emissions over the next 30 years, if present policies continue.

Making your home more **energy efficient** is an immediate step you can take to reduce CO$_2$ emissions. Friends of the Earth have calculated that domestic **energy saving** could reduce annual UK emissions of CO$_2$ by over 19 million tons. The process of creating nuclear power yields much lower levels of CO$_2$, but it has been shown that, even disregarding the environmental risks of nuclear power, non-nuclear energy efficiency programs are seven times more cost effective than nuclear power use in cutting CO$_2$ emissions.

**Carbon dioxide**
**Carbon monoxide**

**Carbon monoxide (CO)** This deadly poisonous, odorless gas can cause pollution problems indoors. Even at low levels, CO poses a health risk. Symptoms include drowsiness, headaches, and dizziness. At high levels it can cause suffocation: those with heart, lung, and blood disorders are most vulnerable. In the US, CO leaking from faulty gas appliances accounts for around 300 deaths from carbon monoxide poisoning each year.

CO is mainly produced by faulty gas **furnaces** and other **gas** appliances, though it is also present in **wood** and **coal** smoke, and **tobacco** smoke. If gas appliances are not properly adjusted so that fuel fails to burn efficiently, or if the exhaust gases cannot escape because, for example, of a blocked flue, then CO fumes may be given off.
In the home, poorly-ventilated rooms, or tightly-sealed rooms may make any CO build-up worse. Take precau-

tions by ensuring that gas furnaces are ventilated to the outside, chimney flues, grilles, and vents are not blocked, and gas burners are properly adjusted. Have all appliances carefully checked and serviced.

CO is also given off by car exhausts. Never run your car engine in a closed **garage** (p. 48) and make sure rooms situated above garages have particularly good **ventilation**.

**Carbon tetrachloride** A colorless liquid with a distinctive smell, carbon tetrachloride is produced by treating **methane** with **chlorine**. It is used as a **solvent** in waxes, lacquers and rubbing compounds, and as an industrial cleaning agent. Carbon tetrachloride was utilized in early **fire extinguishers**, but discontinued because of toxicity. Now its main use is in the manufacture of **CFCs**, and it has a similarly damaging effect on the **ozone** layer. Carbon tetrachloride is an irritant and a suspected carcinogen. It is unlikely to be found in recent DIY products but check the labels of older products you already own. If they contain this chemical, see **Hazardous waste** for disposal.

**Carbon tetrachloride**
**Carpeting**
**Carpet cleaner**

**Carpeting** The backing of synthetic wall-to-wall carpets, especially those containing **polyester**, is usually finished with **formaldehyde**, a suspected carcinogen. New carpets are treated with **insecticides**, and **wool** varieties may have been treated with **mothproofer**. Choose natural, untreated carpeting backed with **hessian** and a felt, rather than foam underlay. If you are particularly sensitive, steam-clean wool carpets before use. See also **Flooring** for more alternatives to carpets.

**Carpet cleaner** Carpet shampoo may contain **perchloroethylene**, a **solvent** used in **dry cleaning** that causes long-term damage to vital organs and is a suspected carcinogen. Another common ingredient is **naphthalene**, also a suspected carcinogen. A safer way to clean carpets is to steam-clean them using plain water. If this does not remove stains, mix one part of **dishwashing liquid** with two parts of boiling water, cool, whip with a beater, and apply. You can also sprinkle the carpet liberally with **bicarbonate of soda**, leave it on for two hours, or overnight, then vacuum off. Bicarbonate of soda, also acts as a deodorizer. Commercial, nontoxic carpet cleaners are also available. See **Stain remover**.

**Casein** This is a protein found in milk. It is used in some types of water-based **paint** and gives a smooth finish that is washable. You can add artists' pigments to casein paint to create your own colors. See also **Paint, organic**.

**Catalytic converter** A catalytic converter or "cat" is a metal-coated chamber fitted into the exhaust system of a car. It works by provoking a chemical reaction that changes most of the harmful exhaust emissions into less harmful ones. Car engines emit three major classes of pollutant gases: **carbon monoxide (CO), nitric oxide (NO)** and **nitrogen dioxide ($NO_2$)**, and **hydrocarbons**. A two-way "cat" cuts harmful emissions by about half, reducing CO and hydrocarbon, but not NO or $NO_2$. A three-way "cat" reduces all three classes of pollutant gases by around 90 percent, changing them into **carbon dioxide**, nitrogen, and **water**. Carbon dioxide is, of course, a greenhouse gas so even cars fitted with "cats" will still contribute to the **greenhouse effect**. Converters are also categorized as "controlled" or "uncontrolled". In the first type, a sensor in the exhaust system monitors gas levels and adjusts the air/fuel ratio so that the converter is operating at maximum efficiency. The "uncontrolled" type is less expensive but has no monitoring system. Cars fitted with convertors will not run on leaded fuel. Since 1975, all new cars in the US must by law be fitted with a catalytic converter.

A converter will normally last for the lifetime of your car. It will not significantly impair performance and it is estimated that fuel consumption will only increase by between 1 and 3 percent. This small sacrifice for cleaner air is considered to be well worth its additional expense.

**Caustic soda** See **Sodium hydroxide**.

**Cellophane** This is a natural, non-synthetic form of **packaging**. It is made from **cellulose**, a plant material, and is **biodegradable**.

**Cellulose** A fibrous material found in the cell walls of plants and trees, cellulose is widely used in the textile industry to make **rayon**. Natural cellulose sponges for household cleaning are widely available, and a type of **insulation** material using cellulose fibers has been developed for walls and roofs.

Casein
Catalytic converter
Caustic soda
Cellophane
Cellulose

**Cement** A mixture of chalk or limestone, and clay, cement is combined with sand and used as a base coat for interior walls before a top coat of **plaster** is applied. A sand and cement combination is also used to make concrete and mortar for paths, drives, and walls, often with the addition of aggregate. Inside the home, **grout** for tiles is often cement-based. Cement is an irritant, and prolonged contact with wet cement can burn your skin. Take precautions by wearing a dust mask when mixing concrete or mortar, and consider wearing gloves to protect skin when using cement-based grout. **Asbestos**-based cement boarding for walls, and asbestos piping and corrugated roofing, are being phased out. See also **Asbestos**.

Cement
Central heating

**Central heating** Heating and hot water account for at least 80 percent of domestic fuel consumption. Heating your home more efficiently results in savings on fuel bills, while the reduction in the amount of **energy** consumed uses up fewer nonrenewable resources and causes less pollution. An average electric central heating system in a three bedroom house uses 14,000 KW hours of electricity a year and this produces 15.4 tons of **carbon dioxide ($CO_2$)**. **Gas** central heating produces 40 percent less and is 30 percent more efficient. A **gas-condensing boiler** is the most fuel and cost efficient of hydronic **boilers**, achieving up to 20 percent more efficiency than standard models. Be sure, however, that gas boilers are regularly serviced: incorrectly adjusted boilers may emit hazardous **carbon monoxide**.

For maximum efficiency and **energy conservation** from your central heating system, turn down thermostats in rooms and on radiators and water heater tanks. Reducing the room temperature by an average of $2^{\circ}$F can save up to eight percent on your fuel bill. If you have a setback or timed thermostat, set it to allow heating to come on half an hour later, or go off half an hour earlier for further savings. Installing sheets of heavy-duty metal foil behind radiators on outside walls reflects heat back into the room, reducing energy loss to the outside. You can also lose heat if you have radiators below **windows** that are overhung by curtains. The heat rises up between radiator and curtain and is lost through the window. Shorten your curtains or widen the windowsills to reflect back the heat. If you are installing central heating, site radiators on inside walls away from windows. For best results, all these economy measures must be combined with good **insulation**.

On a wider scale, community heating systems such as district heating stations, are an efficient and economic method of heating homes. Incinerating domestic **waste** is another method of generating heat that could become more important in the future. See also **Furnace**.

**CFCs** This acronym refers to **chlorofluorocarbons**, gases containing chlorine that may still be found as propellants in a very small proportion of **aerosols**, in blown-foam **packaging**, in home **insulation** materials, as coolants and insulating materials in **refrigerators** and **air-conditioning** systems, in the electronics industry for cleaning circuit boards, and for **dry cleaning**.

CFC gases float into the upper atmosphere where they inflict severe damage on the protective **ozone** layer: a single spray can containing CFCs is capable of destroying 3.3 tons of ozone. One atom of chlorine alone can destroy as many as 100,000 molecules of ozone. CFCs are identified by numbers and refrigerators contain CFCs 11 and 12, two of the most damaging CFCs. The US Environmental Protection Agency has predicted that if no controls are placed on emissions of CFCs and **halons**, found in some types of **fire extinguisher**, there will be over 150 million extra cases of skin cancer in white US citizens born before 2075. CFCs are also one of the four main gases that together are held to be responsible for the **greenhouse effect**. CFCs break down very slowly and can remain in the atmosphere for many years. This means that even if CFCs are phased out there will still be excessively high levels of chlorine in the atmosphere. In the UK, Friends of the Earth predict a four-fold increase in atmospheric chlorine unless stringent measures are adopted. Other ozone-damaging chemicals are halons, **carbon tetrachloride**, and **1,1,1-trichloroethane (methyl chloroform)**, one of the most widely used **solvents**. CFCs with very low ozone depletion potential are now being manufactured.

### Steps that you can take to reduce CFC levels

- Ban aerosols that use CFC propellants from your home. Buy non-CFC varieties or, even better, use a **pump-action spray**.
- Be sure when insulating your roof that insulation material is not the CFC-containing, rigid, foamed **polyurethane**

or extruded **polystyrene**. Use alternatives such as **vermiculite** chips or **cellulose** fiber.

- Avoid packaging and food and drink containers made from polystyrene.
- If you are planning to buy a new refrigerator, consider waiting until new CFC-free models are available. If you need a new one immediately, choose a model that uses coolants with very low ozone depletion potential. Do not allow your old refrigerator to be simply scrapped as this is a sure way to release the CFCs locked inside it. Ask the manufacturer or your local repair contractor to reclaim and recycle the CFC coolants in your old model. Some retailers also offer this service.
- Do not buy **stain remover, correction fluid**, or **adhesives** that contain 1,1,1-trichloroethane.
- Choose halon-free fire extinguishers.

**Chimney** Exhaust gases and smoke from heating appliances may re-enter the room when chimney flues are blocked by soot, debris or loose bricks. Gases, smoke, and soot contain such harmful pollutants as **carbon monoxide**, and inadequate **ventilation**, especially in tightly-sealed rooms, exacerbates the problem. Be sure that your chimney has a good draft, that there are no cracks or blockages, and have it regularly swept.

**Chipboard** This type of **compositeboard** is popular for **kitchen** units (p. 16), **flooring**, and such DIY jobs in the home as shelving. It is also widely employed for household fixtures. Chipboard is manufactured from waste wood chips and fresh **timber**, usually **softwood**. The chips are bound together with a **formaldehyde** resin, then pressed into sheets at high temperatures. Formaldehyde, a suspected carcinogen, can **outgas** indoors, especially when new. Seal chipboard with a natural **varnish** to prevent formaldehyde fumes from escaping. For fixtures, choose a **sustainable timber**, or for flooring, consider a cement-bonded chipboard that is formaldehyde-free.

**Chlorinated hydrocarbons** Chemical compounds that contain carbon, hydrogen, and **chlorine** are known as chlorinated hydrocarbons. Some in common use include such **solvents** as **trichloroethylene**, and insecticides such as **lindane**. See individual entries.

**Chlorine** This poisonous greenish-yellow gas can cause irritation to eyes, throat, and lungs when inhaled in small quantities. Breathing in larger quantities of the gas fills the lungs with fluid, causing death. Chlorine is one of the most widely-used bleaching agents, and an ingredient of many brands of household **bleach**. Poisonous chlorine (also known as **chloramine**) gas can be produced if bleach or bleach-based liquids, such as **toilet cleaner**, are accidentally combined with cleaning products containing **ammonia**. Never mix cleaning products: inhaling this gas could prove fatal. Chlorine is also used industrially to bleach **paper** products, and this process results in highly toxic compounds known as **dioxins**.

Some municipal **water** authorities use chlorine extensively to kill bacteria in **drinking water** supplies and to disinfect swimming pools. It gives water an unpleasant taste plus a distinctive smell. Some people have allergic reactions to chlorine: for example, skin and hair problems after swimming. In January 1990, water supplied to the Tyneside area of the UK was contaminated with **phenols** – **aromatic compounds** used as disinfectants. It was then treated with chlorine before being piped to consumers. This combination of chemicals turned some of the phenols into chlorophenols and there is limited evidence that these substances cause cancer in humans. The ability of chlorine to react with other chemicals in water in this way and produce potentially carcinogenic substances has raised fears about the safety of chlorinating water supplies at all. A domestic **water filter** can remove or significantly reduce free chlorine and chlorine compounds in drinking water.

**Chlorine bleach** See **Bleach**.

**Chloramine** See **Chlorine**.

**Chlorofluorocarbons** See **CFCs**.

**Cigarette smoke** See **Tobacco smoke**.

**Citric acid** This acid, present in citrus fruits, is commonly found in **descaler** for the **kettle**, **bath**, and sink. It is relatively mild and can be bought in powdered form. It may, however, irritate the skin and eyes of sensitive people. See **Descaler** for safer, acid-free alternatives.

**Cleaners** See individual entries, such as **Bleach**, **Drain cleaner**, **Scouring powder**, and **Toilet cleaner**.

**Clingfilm** Concern has been expressed over the plasticizers added to **PVC** to make clingfilm food wrap. Plasticizers are suspected carcinogens and can migrate from food wrap into food. There is a higher risk with warm food, and, because the plasticizers are more soluble in fat, with such fatty foods as cheese or meat. Avoid wrapping fatty or warm food in clingfilm and do not use it with food that is to be heated in a **microwave**. A safer alternative is to opt for brands of clingfilm without plasticizers. Look for labels that state "non PVC" or "plasticizer-free". You can also place food in a bowl and stretch the film over the top so that it does not come into direct contact with the food. Because clingfilm is not **biodegradable**, it presents disposal problems, and PVC is particularly difficult to recycle. Choose instead greaseproof wax **paper** or **cellophane**, and store food in **glass** or earthenware containers.

**Coal** Coal is a nonrenewable **fossil fuel** that will inevitably become scarcer and more expensive to mine. The mining of coal also poses environmental problems. When burned, the high levels of **carbon dioxide ($CO_2$)** released make coal the biggest contributor to the **greenhouse effect** and **acid rain**. The coal-fired power stations that are the main source of our domestic electricity supply are the major producers of $CO_2$. Coal fires are not an efficient form of household heating since about 80 percent of the heat is lost up the **chimney**. Conserving **energy** in your home would reduce demand, save on fuel bills, and contribute towards the reduction of both $CO_2$ emissions and acid rain. See also **Energy saving**.

**Cockroach control** As an alternative to toxic **insecticides**, make your own cockroach trap or powder. For the trap, place pieces of banana, apple, or banana peel inside an upright jar and grease the rim. A ruler or piece of wood propped against the jar will enable the insects to climb up but the grease will prevent them getting out. A mixture of 1 part flour, 1 part cocoa powder, and 4 parts **borax**, or equal parts **bicarbonate of soda** and sugar, will quickly kill cockroaches. If you are using the borax mixture, make sure that it is out of the reach of small children.

**Coffee filters** Most **paper** used for filters has been whitened with **chlorine bleach**, enabling harmful **dioxins** to leach into your coffee. Choose unbleached filters, reusable cloth filters, or invest in a coffee-making machine with a metal filter.

**Coir** This plant fiber is made from the coarse "hair" around coconuts. Coir is a hard-wearing, natural choice for mats and flooring in areas where durability is a priority. It may also be found in fiber mattresses.

**Combustion gases** Fuels used in the home for heating and cooking release pollutants that can contaminate indoor air. These include **carbon dioxide**, **carbon monoxide**, **nitric oxide**, **nitrogen oxide**, and **sulphur dioxide**. Be certain appliances are regularly serviced and that there is adequate **ventilation** in your home.

**Compositeboard** The most popular compositeboard used in the home is **chipboard**. See also **Board**.

**Condensation** Condensation is caused by a build up of moisture in the air of inadequately ventilated areas and occurs when moist air hits cold surfaces. **Kitchens** (p. 16) and **bathrooms** (p. 80) may be particularly affected, as well as rooms with a **bottled gas heater**. Left unchecked, condensation allows **mold** and other bacteria to flourish, and these may trigger allergies as well as creating ideal conditions for wet rot. Open windows, install heating to warm the interior surfaces, install extractor fans, and make sure that appliances are vented. See also **Moisture**.

**Conservatory** A conservatory, or sunspace, has become a popular additional feature of many homes. Ideal as a family room or for growing indoor plants, an alternative use for a conservatory is as a solar collector to provide extra heating. Built on to the south-facing or sunny side of the house, the large expanse of glazing, often **double glazing**, traps the sun's heat, especially if it is built on solid masonry walls and floor. It also takes in warmer air via open **windows** or vents. By opening doors in to the **living room** (p. 122) you have an additional source of heat in cooler periods. At night, to prevent heat loss, insulate the conservatory from the outside, or shut it off from the rest of the house. Although a conservatory can help to reduce heating bills in cooler weather, research has shown that the high cost of installation is difficult to justify on grounds of **energy saving** alone. It is more realistic to look upon the additional warmth your conservatory can supply as a bonus, and consider it primarily as an extra room with an excellent supply of natural light. See **Solar heating** for ways of using solar energy for heating.

**Cookware** The metal **aluminum** can leach into food from pans and cookware, especially if such acidic foods as tomatoes are being cooked. This may pose a health risk, since aluminum in the diet is thought to be linked with Alzheimer's disease, or premature senility. Older enameled pans and casserole dishes, too, may contain toxic **cadmium** and if these are worn and chipped, cadmium may leach into your food. Avoid **non-stick** pans, especially those coated with plastic. These pans may give off harmful fumes when hot, and particles from non-stick plastic coatings will flake off in your food as the coating is worn down. Cook with stainless steel, cast-iron, or new enamel: all of these materials are durable and cast-iron pans, in particular, cook food very evenly and are virtually non-stick. Lightly oiled, they last a lifetime. A stainless-steel **pressure cooker** is also a good investment since it will cook food quickly and save **energy**.

**Cooking foil** Made from **aluminum**, the manufacture of this metal is extremely energy intensive, and some of the raw material, bauxite, used to make the metal is mined in rainforest areas. Wrap food and cook with greaseproof paper instead, or use the wrappers from butter. Aluminum foil, however, can be used to save energy in the home. Put it behind radiators sited on outside walls, shiny side outermost, to reflect back heat.

**Cork** Cork consists of the outer bark of the cork oak tree. It is a renewable natural resource, since the bark can be harvested every eight to ten years without damaging the tree, and all of it is used. Cork is an excellent insulation material, for heat as well as noise, and it is resistant to rot and **mold**. Wall and floor tiles made from compressed cork granules are widely available. Cork board can also be used to insulate roofs, floors and walls. Avoid tiles that are

**Cookware**
**Cooking foil**
**Cork**

backed with **vinyl** and when affixing tiles choose natural **adhesives** such as **lignin paste** or a special adhesive available from **organic paint** suppliers. Cork generally needs no finish, but if you are using it for **flooring**, seal the tiles with a natural **varnish**. Cork is also used to make **linoleum**.

**Correction fluid** Most correction fluid is solvent-based. The **solvent** commonly used is **1,1,1-trichloroethane**, a substance that is harmful by inhalation, can seriously damage the eyes, and cause dizziness, and is capable of destroying **ozone**. When using correction fluid, avoid breathing in the vapor and always replace the cap after use. Choose safer, water-based products that do not harm the environment.

**Cosmetics** Many cosmetics companies rely on **animal testing** for their products. If you object to this practice, choose **cruelty free** brands that are guaranteed not to have been tested on animals.

**Cotton** See **Fabrics**.

**Creosote** Used to preserve exterior **wood**, especially fencing, creosote is toxic if swallowed, inhaled, or absorbed through the skin. It has a pungent odor, contains a high percentage of **phenols**, and is carcinogenic. When using creosote wear gloves, boots, protect your eyes, and try not to inhale the vapor. Keep children and pets well away from treated surfaces until they are completely dry. Avoid creosote and see **Wood preservative** for safer alternatives.

**Cresol** This **organic** compound is commonly found in household **disinfectant**. Cresol is toxic if it is inhaled or absorbed through the skin, and may cause allergic reactions. See **Disinfectant** for alternatives.

**Cruelty-free** Cosmetics and **toiletries** may display this term on their labels. At present, however, it has no standardized definition. Some "cruelty-free" products contain ingredients that have not been tested on animals in the last five years; others have not been tested on animals since 1976. Some manufacturers use the term when the product itself has not been tested on animals, although its ingredients might have been. At present a labeling scheme exists run by the British Association for the Abolition of Vivisection (BUAV). Under this scheme a "white rabbit" logo may be displayed by companies or suppliers that have not tested either ingredients or the finished product on animals in the last five years. New EC rulings on the safety of cosmetics, however, are in preparation, and ingredients not tested since 1976 may have to be tested again.

**Cyanoacrylates** This group of chemicals is commonly found in "superglues" – fast-acting **adhesives** that bond in seconds. Cyanoacrylates are powerful irritants that may cause allergic reactions. Avoid inhaling the vapor and on no account spill these glues on your skin. See **Adhesives** for alternatives.

**Cypermethrin** This synthetic insecticide belongs to the same family as **permethrin** and is commonly used indoors as a **wood preservative**. A suspected animal carcinogen, exposure to cypermethrin can result in dermatitis, pins and needles, and hay fever-like symptoms. See **Wood preservative** for alternatives.

**Cyanoacrylates**
**Cypermethrin**

**Damp proof course (DPC)** The DPC is an impermeable layer near the base of the walls of the house. It acts as a barrier against the moisture that rises up naturally from the ground, preventing it from rising any higher up the walls and into the house. In the UK, the first damp courses appeared in properties built after 1875. If you want to install or replace a DPC, you can consider two types of barrier: the first consists of a "physical" layer, like a termite shield, of **aluminum**, **lead**, **bitumen**, **felt**, or **plastic**, that is inserted into the wall after a course of mortar has been removed; the second type consists of a chemical **damp proofing fluid** that is injected into holes drilled in the masonry and saturates the bricks.

**Damp proofing fluid** To make buildings damp- or **moisture**-proof, brick and stonework immediately above ground level are injected with a chemical damp-proofing fluid. The fluid usually consists of waterproof **silicone** in a flammable **solvent** base. The solvent emits harmful vapors, and the fluid may irritate the skin. As a general precaution, vacate rooms directly above treated areas until the vapors have dispersed. When carrying out treatment yourself, wear protective clothing and keep the fluid away from sources of ignition.

**Dehumidifier** This electrical appliance extracts excess moisture from the air in areas where **moisture** or **conden-**

**sation** is a problem. Dehumidifiers use a fan to draw in moist air that is then cooled and the resultant water from the air is collected in a container. The dry air is warmed and then recirculated into the room, providing an effective means of background heating. You can use a dehumidifier to help dry out rooms where there has been severe water penetration, or to keep a holiday home or a camper dry. Dehumidifiers can also be used to dry out newly plastered walls, and they will protect books or other possessions stored in a damp **basement** (p. 50). Dehumidifiers must be emptied regularly to prevent the formation of mold in the containers. Installing a dehumidifier is not, however, a remedy for such problems as penetrating moisture or rising moisture. You must tackle the cause of the problem and cure it quickly. See **Moisture**.

**De-icer** The active ingredient of de-icer is **methanol**, an **alcohol** that is also commonly used in **paint stripper**. Methanol is a highly toxic **solvent** with harmful vapors. Continued exposure, even to small doses, damages the optic nerve. Do not inhale de-icer, and take care not to spill it on your skin as it will be readily absorbed into your body. De-icer is also highly flammable so keep it away from sources of ignition. A safer alternative for windshields and windows is a hand scraper. You can also use a salt solution, while rubbing a halved raw potato over the windshield will prevent reicing.

**De-icer**
**Demand switch**
**Deodorant**

**Demand switch** This device, which originated in Germany, isolates some or all electrical circuits in the home, switching off the current once it is no longer needed. It is particularly recommended for rooms where babies or small children sleep and for **bedrooms** (p.112) generally.

**Deodorant** Common ingredients of deodorants are chemicals that kill bacteria, and artificial fragrance. Deodorants that also have an **antiperspirant** action contain **aluminum chlorohydrate**, a compound that blocks the pores. These products can irritate your skin, especially if it is broken, and aerosol varieties may contain **CFCs** or **hydrocarbon** propellants. Choose plant-based roll-on deodorant, or make your own by diluting an **essential oil** in water or vegetable oil. Lavender oil is both refreshing and antiseptic: dilute 20 drops in one and a half ounces of vegetable oil or the same quantity of water. **Bicarbonate of soda** patted on after washing also makes a good deodorant.

**Descaler** For removing the limescale, or calcium, deposited in your **kettle**, steam iron, **bath**, sink, **toilet**, and **shower** head, two kinds of commercial descaler are available: a strong **formic acid-**, **sulphamic acid-**, or **phosphoric acid-**based formula, and a milder **citric acid** formula. The corrosive acids in the first type of descaler are toxic and may damage surfaces, while formic acid emits vapors that will irritate the eyes. Accidental spillage of phosphoric acid could cause serious skin and eye injuries. When using descalers containing any of these three types of acid, avoid inhaling the fumes, guard against spills, and wear gloves to protect your skin. Citric acid is milder and thought to be suitable for culinary purposes, but it may irritate the skin and eyes of sensitive people.

**Descaler**

   A safer alternative is to choose from a range of nontoxic commercial descalers that are acid-free, non-corrosive, and **biodegradable**. You can also make your own kettle descaler from a mixture of white **vinegar**, diluted in the same amount of **water**, but do not overfill the kettle. Bring the kettle to the boil, switch it off, and leave it for one to two hours. If the kettle is badly coated, leave the solution in overnight, but always rinse thoroughly to get rid of the smell. You can also buy citric acid powder from a drug store or pharmacist. Add two and a half ounces to a kettle of boiled water, reheating once if some scale still remains. **Washing soda** is another good kettle descaler; but do not use it on **aluminum** kettles. Regular descaling of your kettle will save you **energy**, since a calcium-coated kettle takes longer to boil the water. To remove scale deposits from the toilet bowl, pour in undiluted white vinegar, leave overnight, and finish off with a brush the next morning. Use concentrated lemon juice or **borax** for removing scale from baths, sinks, and taps. To reduce scale build-up in kettles and steam irons, always fill them with water from a **water filter**.

   If you live in an area where the water is particularly hard and scale regularly accumulates in **pipes**, radiators, and the water heater, your heating bills will be substantially higher. One solution is to have a commercial scale-reducer fitted to the pipes that supply your **shower** and central-hydronic heating **boiler**. Scale-reducers are cartridges containing crystals that help prevent the formation of limescale. The cartridges must be replaced at two- or three-monthly intervals, however.

**Detergent** See **Laundry powder**.

**Diapers** Washable, terry-towelling diapers have now generally been replaced with the disposable kind. In 1989, however, questions were raised about the acceptability of disposables from both health and environmental points of view. Environmentalists expressed concern that, due to the **chlorine bleach** used on the wood pulp that makes up the padding, diapers were contaminated with dangerous **dioxins**. In response to consumer concern, leading manufacturers switched to a non-chlorine bleaching process, and safer, off-white disposables are now widely available. From an environmental perspective, the 3.5 billion disposable diapers used each year in the UK alone result in major **waste** disposal problems. The **plastic** backing is not, on the whole, **biodegradable**, although in some brands it does biodegrade to some extent. Concern has also been expressed at the insanitary practice of dumping large quantities of soiled diapers in landfills. In the US, manufacturers are experimenting with **recycling** the wood pulp padding in disposables.

The best alternatives to disposable diapers are terry-towelling diapers plus reusable diaper covers made from **wool**. Terry diapers are time-consuming to wash but work out cheaper than disposables. They are also less likely to give your child diaper rash. Soak terry-towelling diapers in mild **borax** solution (2 tsps/10ml to 7.5 litres of water) to disinfect them and to reduce stains and smells. Detachable wool diaper covers are washable and will last through four to six diaper changes.

**Diazinon** This **insecticide** may be the active ingredient in flea collars for cats. It is rapidly absorbed through animals' skin and is harmful to them since it causes birth defects in laboratory animals. Diazinon is an irritant to human skin and eyes. See **Flea powder** for safe alternatives.

**1,2-dibromoethane** This ingredient of leaded **gasoline** is added to prevent lead particles building up in the engine. It is carcinogenic and an irritant to skin and eyes. Keep it

Attached garages are a source of hazardous fumes, such as **carbon monoxide**. Garages situated underneath, or next to another room pose a particular danger to health if ducts from the garage to the house are left unsealed. Another health hazard in areas of granite rock, is the radioactive and carcinogenic **radon** gas entering your home via the basement. Radon can seep from the subsoil and in through cracks in basement floors and walls. **Moisture** in the basement can also be a serious problem.

### Garage

**Car** Approximately a quarter of the US's total **carbon dioxide ($CO_2$)** output can be directly attributed to motor vehicles. Increased $CO_2$ emissions are the primary cause of the **greenhouse effect**. Motor vehicles contribute significantly to air pollution since car exhausts discharge such hazardous contaminants as **benzene**, carbon monoxide, **lead**, **nitric oxide**, and **nitrogen dioxide**. In addition, when exhaust gases react with sunlight, harmful **ozone** smog is produced at ground level. Minimize the health problems and environmental damage associated with cars by driving less, carpooling, switching to unleaded **gasoline**, and driving a car with a **catalytic converter**.

**Gasoline** Leaded gasoline puts the health of children at risk. Even low levels of lead can impair children's mental abili-

ties, while prolonged exposure to lead can affect the nervous system, kidneys, and the reproductive system of adults. Use unleaded gasoline and guard against fire, since gasoline is highly flammable.

**Exhaust gases** Motor vehicles are responsible for 85-90 percent of US carbon monoxide levels. Carbon monoxide is a poisonous gas and high doses can be fatal. Never run the car engine in a garage, especially if it is situated underneath or adjacent to another room.

Benzene is also highly toxic and can cause cancer; and nitrogen oxides irritate the lungs. Do not breathe in gasoline vapors especially when filling up your car, and drive a

1 **Protective clothing**
2 **Bicycles**
3 **Unleaded gasoline**
4 **Radial tires**
5 **Car with catalytic converter**
6 **Good ventilation**
7 **Reused glass storage jars**
8 **Workbench**
9 **Manual tools for gardening**
10 **Safety goggles**
11 **Hand tools**
12 **Dust mask**
13 **Protective gloves**
14 **Storage bins**

vehicle with a three-way catalytic converter to cut emissions of pollutants.

**Brake and clutch lining** Toxic **asbestos** is traditionally used in brake and clutch linings. Ideally, have linings replaced professionally. If you are replacing them yourself, wear a dust mask. Wrap old linings and any loose particles in a sealed bag and treat as **hazardous waste**. Choose new linings that are asbestos-free.

**Battery acid** The acid used in batteries is **sulphuric acid**, a corrosive and poisonous substance. It leaves deposits around battery terminals that are also toxic. Wear gloves and handle batteries with care. Do

not dump old batteries; take them to a garage or dispose of them as hazardous waste.

**Engine oil, antifreeze, dry start, deicer** Engine oil may contain lead. It can also irritate the skin, so protect your hands by using a barrier cream. Take used engine oil to a service station or reclamation center for **recycling**. Do not pour it down the drain or set fire to it. Antifreeze contains a sweet-tasting, irritant **solvent**. Keep it well out of the reach of children and off your skin. Dry start and de-icer contain solvents that are toxic by inhalation. Only use dry start and de-icer outside and buy a scraper to remove ice from your windshield.

**Garage & basement**

**Spray paint** This contains such solvents as **xylene**, an irritant that can cause drowsiness. Because it is in spray form it is more easily inhaled. **Aerosol** sprays may contain **CFCs**. Wear a dust mask when spraying, or choose products that can be applied with a brush and use in well ventilated areas only.

**Tires** Of the 250 million tires discarded each year in the US, 35 percent could be remolded or recycled. In practice, **recycling** facilities are scarce and only 9 percent of tires are reused. Tires can also be burnt to produce **energy** in power stations. Make sure that you get the most out of your existing tires by keeping them properly inflated and choosing the durable radial variety. This will also give you a six to eight percent saving on gasoline.

**Oily rags**, **grease**, **oil** and products containing solvents, all pose a serious fire hazard. Store them away safely in metal trays or bins.

## Basement

**Radon** A naturally occurring radioactive gas that causes cancer, radon can seep into your home from underground rocks, especially in areas with granite beds. Radon is formed by the decay of uranium, and, because it is heavier than air, it tends to collect in basements and low-lying areas. The US EPA estimates that up to 10 million homes may have radon levels above the 4 picocuries

1 Nontoxic cleaners
2 Chest freezer
3 Biodegradable, phosphate-free washing powder
4 Low-energy washing machine
5 Vent
6 Sorted waste for recycling
7 Wicker or cane baskets
8 Window for ventilation and light
9 Clothes line
10 Rendered walls
11 Lagged pipework
12 Sealed floor

per liter of air safety limit. Government grants and low-interest loan programs may be available to make homes with levels above this limit radon proof, so if you are concerned, get your local Environmental Health Office to provide a source of radon testing. To prevent radon penetrating your basement, seal all cracks in the basement walls, floor, and ceiling. Be sure that there are no gaps around service **pipes**. Good **ventilation** in the basement is essential. Install a fan with a duct to enable the gas to be dispersed outside.

**Moisture** Basements can suffer from rising moisture caused by water penetration and inadequate ventilation. First check that your **damp proof course (DPC)** is not defective. If it is, or if you live in an older house without a DPC, have one installed; the termite shield that's required by code also serves to stop water penetration. If you have a DPC, check from both the outside and the inside that it has not been "bridged" or covered. On the outside, earth can pile up against a wall above the level of the DPC, or rendering on outside walls could have extended too far downward. On the inside, plasterwork may have extended down over the DPC. Always make sure the DPC is not obstructed and that all rendering or interior plasterwork stops above it. You can also waterproof base-ment walls by installing dim-pled plastic sheeting and plas-tering over it, or by rendering with sand and **cement**. If you have a serious moisture prob-lem, you may have to take up the floor and have it relaid incorporating a **polythene** membrane. This membrane would also be effective in keeping out radon.

For deep basements, you may need to dig away the soil from the outer walls and coat them with an impermeable finish before replacing the soil. Also, laying ground drains at foundation level will help relieve water pressure. Alternatively, you can "dry-line" the internal walls by building a new inner masonry wall with a ventilated cavity.

off your skin, do not inhale the fumes, and change to unleaded gasoline.

**Dichlofluanid** This **fungicide** is found in several **wood preservatives** for use in the home. It is an irritant to skin and eyes, and there is some evidence of genetic damage to laboratory animals. Dichlofluanid is harmful to fish, so do not dispose of wood preservative down the drain where it will pollute the water supply. See **Hazardous waste** for disposal and see **Wood preservatives** for safer alternatives.

**Dichlorobenzene** See **Para-dichlorobenzene**.

**Dichloromethane** Known also as **methylene chloride**, dichloromethane is a **chlorinated solvent** that is found in solvent-based **paint stripper** and **varnish** remover. Dichloromethane emits harmful fumes that cause drowsiness and dizziness, and it is a powerful skin irritant. Evidence from the US shows that this chemical is an animal carcinogen and the Consumer Product Safety Commission has designated it a hazardous substance. Use products containing dichloromethane only in well-ventilated conditions, keep it off your skin, and wear gloves. See **Paint stripper** for alternatives.

**Dichlorvos** An **insecticide** commonly used in cat flea collars, dichlorvos is also the active ingredient in solid-block **fly-killer**, and in some **woodworm killer**. An **organophosphate**, dichlorvos works by affecting the nervous system and is extremely hazardous. It is a suspected carcinogen and has been associated with the onset of symptoms resembling multiple sclerosis. The UK Department of the Environment is currently considering banning dichlorvos. See **Flea powder**, **Fly killer** for safe alternatives.

**Diethylene glycol** This **solvent** is an ingredient of some **stain removers** that emits toxic vapors and causes cancer in laboratory animals. Formerly added to **cellophane** food wrapping, the practice was stopped in 1985 when diethylene glycol was found to have migrated into the food.

**Diethyl toluamide (DEET)** This is the common active ingredient of **insect repellent** gels and sprays to keep off gnats and mosquitoes, and is a toxic chemical. Repeated exposure to DEET has led to brain and nervous system damage. Strong solutions absorbed through the skin have also led to severe skin problems. Avoid prolonged use of these insect repellents and do not use them at all on small children. See **Insect repellent** for safer alternatives.

**Dimethoate** Because this **insecticide** is used on many crops in the UK, high levels of dimethoate have been found in drinking **water** there. A suspected carcinogen in the US, the Environmental Protection Agency has banned the use of this chemical. If you live in an agricultural region of heavy **pesticide** use, consider using a **water filter** to reduce levels of dimethoate. See also **Pesticides**.

**Dioxins** This term refers to a group of hazardous chemicals that are produced as a by-product of the industrial **chlorine** bleaching process used on wood pulp for **paper**, **diapers**, and **sanitary protection products**. Dioxins, too, can be released when **PVC** is burnt at insufficiently high temperatures in incineration plants. These chemicals are suspected human carcinogens and established animal carcinogens, causing damage to the reproductive and immune systems and accumulating in fatty tissues. In 1989 a report by the UK Women's Environmental Network raised fears that dioxins could be present in diapers and sanitary wear. As a result many manufacturers changed from chlorine to **oxygen bleach**, and offered alternative, unbleached products. In Sweden more than 95 percent of paper products are now unbleached. Another reason for concern about dioxins is the damage they inflict on the environment. Effluents from manufacturing plants using chlorine bleach seriously contaminate rivers, lakes, and seas.

**Dishpan** Washing dishes under a running tap wastes **water**. Always use a dishpan. Pans made from **plastics** that are red, yellow, or orange in color, however, may contain the toxic heavy metal, **cadmium**. Choose those kitchenware products that are labeled cadmium-free.

**Dishwasher** The most efficient automatic dishwashers use 5.3 gallons of **water** per cycle, less even than the 10.5 gallons used to wash dishes by hand for a family of four. Older models, however, may use up to 16 gallons per cycle and all dishwashers use a good deal of **energy**, both in their manufacture, and in heating water and for drying. You can cut consumption of water and, especially, electricity, by selecting the economy cycle and using the dishwasher only when you have a full load. Some machines require less **dishwasher detergent** than others which means less water pollution. A recent model reuses water heat via a **heat exchanger**, making it more **energy efficient**. For economy, always wash small amounts of dirty dishes by hand.

**Dishwasher detergent** Some powder **detergent** may contain a high percentage of **phosphates**, which are serious water pollutants. Choose instead phosphate-free varieties that are also **biodegradable**. You can also try a mixture of one part **borax** to one part **washing soda**. In hard water areas, these proportions may need adjusting.

**Dishwasher detergent**
**Dishwashing liquid**
**Disinfectant**

**Dishwashing liquid** Dishwashing liquid does not contain **phosphates**, so there is no risk of waterways becoming clogged by algae as a result of using this product. But due to excessive foaming in rivers and lakes in the 1960s, dishwashing liquid is now required by law to break down more completely. Sewage treatment works can remove over 95 percent of the foam from proprietary dishwashing liquids but five percent still remains. **Biodegradable** dishwashing liquids, based on vegetable oils, break down fully and more rapidly than the standard brands made from **petroleum**. Some biodegradable varieties contain natural oils rather than synthetic perfume, and no coloring, so they may be less harsh on your skin as well as healthier for the environment.

**Disinfectant** The active ingredients in products described as disinfectants can range from toxic **phenols** and **cresol**, to milder antiseptics for use on the skin. Brands that do not contain phenol are preferable, but there are safer, nontoxic alternatives. Half a cup of **borax** dissolved in just over 1 gallon of water makes a good all-purpose disinfectant for floors, walls, working surfaces, and sinks. For the **toilet**, pour in white **vinegar** and leave overnight. You can also scent these nontoxic disinfectants by adding a few drops of a naturally antiseptic and deodorizing **essential oil**, such as lavender or pine.

**Distemper** A traditional water-based **paint**, now little used, with good disinfectant properties. Since it is not washable, it is suitable for indoor walls and ceilings in areas where durability is not a problem.

**Dodecylamine** This **fungicide** and mold preventer is commonly found in exterior **paint** and washes. Dodecylamine is an irritant so guard against splashing it into your eyes or on to your skin. Never use products containing this chemical with **ammonia**-based preparations, since powerful ammonia gas will be released.

**Double glazing** Installing double glazing will halve the amount of heat, roughly ten percent, that escapes through **windows**. It is however, extremely expensive to install and may take you as long as 20 years to recoup the initial outlay via lower heating bills. Double glazing is generally considered to be economically unjustifiable in most cases. If your existing windows are sound and have been weatherstripped, hanging heavy curtains is a more cost effective measure. See also **Insulation** and **Weatherstripping**.

**Drain cleaner** The active ingredient of drain cleaners is usually **sodium hydroxide**, commonly known as **caustic soda** or **lye**. This toxic, corrosive chemical is a powerful irritant, contaminates **water** supplies, and is harmful to fish. Do not mix cleaners containing caustic soda with those that are **ammonia**-based: toxic ammonia gas will result. **Bleach** is harmful to bacteria that decompose waste products so do not use it as a drain cleaner. A safe, nontoxic alternative that will not damage the environment is a mixture of half a cup of **bicarbonate of soda**, one cup of **vinegar**, and a **kettle** of boiling **water**. Flush the drain with this mixture, and add more hot water if it is clogged.

**Drinking water** See **Water**.

**Drinks cans** See **Cans**.

**Dry and wet rot** To avoid dry and wet rot, ensure all **timber** is kept dry. If timber becomes wet, eliminate the source of the problem immediately (see **Moisture**), and allow the timber to dry out. Good **ventilation** is essential and you may also need to use a **dehumidifier**. Painting timber with stain, **varnish**, and **paint** is a good preventative measure. Choose microporous and nontoxic products from **organic paint** suppliers and see also **Wood preservative, Timber treatments**.

**Dry cleaning** The dry-cleaning process uses **solvents**, mainly **perchloroethylene (perklone)**, to clean clothes. The fumes given off by perklone are toxic, provoking such symptoms as dizziness, nausea, and even leading to unconsciousness. Long-term exposure to dry-cleaning chemicals has been linked to organ damage and the development of cancer. Dry-cleaning fluid is also hazardous to the environment, since effluents discharged by plants into rivers and seas can contaminate **drinking water** supplies. Recently the dry-cleaning industry has invested in newer machines that use one of the top five most damaging **CFCs**, CFC-113. It is less toxic than perklone, but one molecule alone can destroy 100,000 molecules of **ozone**.

   After dry cleaning, hang clothes outside until the smell has dispersed. Consider hand washing delicate fabrics.

**Dry cleaning**
**Dry start**
**Dual-flush toilet**
**Duvet**

**Dry start** This spray contains a **plastic** material used on car engines to help them start in damp conditions. The plastic is dissolved in a **solvent**, usually **xylene**, that evaporates almost immediately. Solvents are flammable and the vapors are harmful. Do not breathe in the spray and only use this product out of doors. Brands of dry start that do not use **CFC** propellants are widely available. Products that dry out already damp engines by dispersing moisture are also available without CFCs.

**Dual-flush toilet** This **toilet** has two flushes, short and longer. The shorter flush uses around 50 percent less water than a standard toilet. This water-conserving toilet is an economic option, especially with metered supplies.

**Duvet** Pure down duvets, or comforter quilts, are light, warm, and comfortable. If you are allergic to feathers, **cotton**-filled quilts are available. Duvets filled with **polyester** or a polyester mixture do not retain heat or absorb moisture as well as feathers or cotton. See **Bedding**.

**"Easy care"** Found on **fabric** labels, this term, like **"perma-nent press"** and **"non-iron"**, means that the fabric has a **formaldehyde** finish that will not wash out. Formaldehyde is a suspected carcinogen, so avoid fabrics with this label, especially for **bedding**.

**Ebony** This **tropical hardwood** is an endangered **timber**. Avoid products made from ebony unless it can be demon-strated that the **wood** comes from managed plantations. See the list of **sustainable timber** on p. 155 for alternatives.

**EDTA** This compound, ethylene diaminetetra-acetate, is added to some brands of **laundry powder** to stabilize the **bleach** and stop it becoming active while still in the pack-et. It is also used as a water softener instead of **phosphates**. EDTA is an environmental contaminant. It combines with such toxic heavy metals already in the wash **water** as **cadmium**, forming soluble compounds that re-enter drinking water supplies, are taken up by fish, and cannot be broken down. See **Laundry powder** for **biodegradable** alternatives.

**Electric blanket** Studies have shown that the rate of mis-carriage is higher for women who use electric blankets. The electric current may set up **electromagnetic fields** that interfere with cell communication in the body. Use a hot water bottle or a fleece underblanket.

"Easy care"
Ebony
EDTA
Electric blanket

**Electromagnetic fields (EMFs)** It is well known that strong electromagnetic fields operate around overhead power lines, but household electricity cables and the growing numbers of electrical appliances in the home and **home office** (p. 176) lso produce EMFs. Metal, in **bed** frames and bed springs, may also become magnetized, and this increases the strength of EMFs. The cumulative effect of these fields, according to international research, is disruptive of the body's natural electrical impulses. Exposure to EMFs has been linked with damage to the immune system, as well as interference with general development and behavior patterns. These collective symptoms are often termed "electrostress". The nearer you are to electrical appliances, the stronger the fields. Consider taking the following precautions: install a **demand switch** in the **bedroom** (p. 112) and **nursery** (p. 144) to cut off the electric current when it is not needed; use a **neutralizing undersheet** that is thought to shield you from EMFs; avoid using an **electric blanket**; and avoid metal bed frames and beds with metal springs. If you use a **personal computer**, sit as far from the sides and back of the screen as possible, and consider installing a screen that will limit EMFs.

Electromagnetic fields
Elm
Emulsion paint
Energy

**Elm** Grown in the UK, Europe, and North America, elm timber is sustainable. The tougher Dutch varieties of this **hardwood**, however, have been badly hit by disease. See the list of **sustainable timber** on p. 155.

**Emulsion paint** This type of **paint** is water-based rather than oil-based and has a low **solvent** content. **Vinyl**, a **plastic**, is used as a binder in emulsion paint, giving it flexibility and durability. See also **Paint, organic**.

**Energy** Fossil fuel energy resources are in limited supply, yet demand for them is increasing. In about 30 years' time, world oil stocks may be exhausted, while in the UK over 40 percent of North Sea oil supplies have already been used up. As **coal** deposits become harder to mine, prices will rise correspondingly. Nuclear power, however does not appear to be an economic or safe alternative. In early 1990 research in the UK uncovered a potential link between radiation exposure of workers at the Sellafield nuclear reprocessing plant and leukemia in their children. Radioactive waste is dangerous and no acceptable waste-management system has yet been developed. Building and running nuclear reactors also entails massive expenditure, and reserves of uranium may last only for another hundred years. All nuclear and fossil-fuel forms of energy are detrimental to the environment, but **fossil fuels**, particularly coal burned in power stations, are the worst contributors to **acid rain** and the **greenhouse effect**. Although "clean coal technology" exists, investment has not so far been forthcoming in many industrial nations, and currently it is **gas** that is the most cost-efficient source of energy and the least environmentally polluting, although gas leakage from mains can be a major contributor to the greenhouse effect. This situation may change when more resources are channelled into developing renewable sources of energy – wind turbines, solar power, wave and tidal power. Wind power is the cheapest, and Denmark and California already have successful "wind farms".

In response to the twin threats of dwindling energy resources and damage to the environment, the best option, until renewables are sufficiently developed, is to use **energy-efficient** forms of heating and appliances in the home, combined with general **energy-saving** measures. Energy also includes fuel for motor vehicles, which accounts for over a quarter of all energy consumption.

**Energy efficient**

**Energy efficient** Improving the energy efficiency of the home, and using such energy-efficient appliances as **refrigerators** and **light bulbs,** will result in lower fuel usage and lower fuel bills. And, since a reduced demand for energy means decreased **carbon dioxide($CO_2$)** emissions, energy efficiency is an obvious way to slow down the greenhouse effect. In the US, Australia, Sweden, and Denmark, investment in energy efficiency programs has been forthcoming, while the EC is helping to fund research into energy efficiency in Germany and Spain. No such investment programs exist in the UK where more than a third of the annual $CO_2$ output is said to be attributable to the electricity industry.

The US already has comprehensive appliance standards laws, and in Europe there are models of such household appliances as the refrigerators that use considerably less electricity a year than standard appliances. See also **Central heating** and **Energy Saving**.

**Energy saving** The following measures will make your home more energy efficient, cut fuel bills, and help to reduce the environmental impact of the fuel industries.

### Steps you can take to save energy
• Insulate walls and attic, **weatherstrip windows** and doors. Hang heavy curtains and draw them at dusk.
• Be sure your water heater is properly insulated.
• Turn down thermostats by $2^\circ$F and set **central heating** to come on half an hour later, and go off half an hour earlier if you have a setback or timed thermostat. Consider installing a **gas condensing boiler** or **furnace**.
• Install heavy-duty metal foil behind radiators that are situated against outside walls to reflect back heat. For radiators beneath windows, stop heat from escaping by making sure that your curtains do not overhang the radiator. You can also widen windowsills over radiators or fit valances at the top of the window.
• Use energy-efficient appliances and **low-energy bulbs**. Turn off unnecessary appliances and lights.
• Use your car less. Share rides and make more use of public transport.

Energy saving
Engine oil
Enzymes
Epoxy resin

**Engine oil** Used engine oil may contain **lead**, so do not burn it or pour it down the drain. Keep it off your skin since the chemical additives it contains are irritants. Engine oil is suitable for **recycling**. Take it to a service station or reclamation center.

**Enzymes** These substances, produced by living cells, digest protein and starch. They help to dissolve stains and are found in **laundry powder** labeled **biological**. Enzymes have produced such allergic reactions as dermatitis and have been associated with respiratory problems. See **Laundry powder** for enzyme-free alternatives.

**Epoxy resin** This synthetic resin is used as an **adhesive**. It is produced by combining compounds containing specially grouped oxygen atoms with **phenols**. Epoxy resin also contains a curing agent and a hardener, and comes in two parts. Both parts are severe skin irritants, and the hardening epoxy part emits harmful vapors. Once mixed, however, the adhesive is safe. Only use epoxy resin in well-ventilated conditions and keep it off your skin. Safer alternatives are water-based adhesives, or organic adhesives available from suppliers of **organic paint**.

**Essential oil** These volatile compounds that occur naturally in the leaves or flowers of scented plants, are used by professional aromatherapists for their powers of healing and relaxation. They are also easy to use at home. The oils, or essences, can be rapidly absorbed via inhalation or through the skin. They work by stimulating the sense of smell and the nerve endings in the skin, and have proven therapeutic properties – both physical and emotional. Essential oils are highly concentrated so you need only a few drops. If you use them on your skin they *must* be diluted: 20 drops in one and a half ounces of vegetable oil. Use sandalwood in incensors and vaporizers, or simply put a few drops in a saucer of water in a warm place to create a soothing evening atmosphere. Lavender oil, recommended for burns, is another excellent relaxant. In common with lemon and pine, it is also naturally disinfectant and any of these three oils can be use in the **bathroom** (p. 80) and **toilet** to cleanse and deodorize. Cedar and rosewood oil added to **polish** give furniture a pleasant, fresh smell, and melissa was traditionally used to scent **beeswax** polish. When buying essential oils, choose only pure, undiluted, natural oils, not synthetic varieties that have already been diluted.

**Essential oil**
**Ethanol**
**Ethyl acetate**
**Ethylene glycol**

**Ethanol** This colorless liquid is the intoxicating ingredient in alcoholic drinks. Ethanol is mainly used as a **solvent** in some DIY products and in cosmetics. Methylated spirit and isopropyl or rubbing alcohol both contain ethanol. Avoid breathing in the vapor from products containing ethanol and guard against fire, since it is highly flammable. Ethanol is also used as a fuel for vehicles in Brazil.

**Ethyl acetate** A **solvent** used in lacquers and nail varnish, ethyl acetate emits a vapor that may irritate the respiratory system. Frequent exposure may also damage the eyes. Ethyl acetate is flammable so take precautions against fire, and only use in well-ventilated conditions. See **Varnish** for alternatives.

**Ethylene glycol** This active ingredient in **antifreeze** is a sweet-tasting **solvent** which is harmful if swallowed or inhaled, and can irritate the skin. Keep products containing this solvent out of the reach of children. See also **Propylene glycol**.

**Ethylene glycol acetate** Used as a **solvent** in cellulose **paint**, ethylene glycol acetate may irritate the skin, and the vapors can be harmful. Only use this type of paint in well ventilated conditions, and see **Paint, organic** for safe alternatives.

**Exhaust gases** Vehicle exhausts discharge pollutant gases into the air that are health risks, and contribute either to **acid rain,** or the **greenhouse effect,** or both. Emission of these gases – **carbon monoxide, hydrocarbons** (including carcinogenic **benzene**), **nitric oxide**, and **nitrogen oxide** – are cut by 90 percent in cars that use a **catalytic converter**.

Ethylene glycol
acetate
Exhaust gases
Extractor fan

**Extractor fan** To remove moist air, reduce **condensation**, and introduce fresh air supplies into the **bathroom** (p. 80) and **kitchen** (p. 16), install an extractor fan. Solar-powered **ventilation** units are a good **energy-saving** choice.

**Fabrics** In the home fabrics usually fall into three categories: natural fibers, synthetics, and natural/synthetic mixtures. The most popular natural fibers are **cotton** and **wool**; synthetics may be based on a polymer such as **polyester** or **acrylic**; while **poly-cotton** and wool/acrylic blends are mixtures of the two. Virtually all cotton has been grown using **pesticides** and is then whitened with **bleach** before dyeing. Cotton labeled **"easy-care"**, **"perma-nent press"**, or **"non-iron"**, plus poly-cotton, have been treated with **formaldehyde**, a suspected carcinogen that binds to the fabric and will not wash out. **Fire-retardant** finishes for fabrics also use a formaldehyde compound. Most synthetic fabrics are produced from non-renewable resources and their manufacture is energy intensive, accounting, it is estimated, for 23,000 barrels of oil a day worldwide. Unlike natural fibers, synthetics are not **biodegradable**. They also have poor breathing qualities, so in summer they leave you feeling sticky. In winter their poor thermal qualities mean that they retain very little of your body heat. Wool for **carpeting** has usually been treat-ed with pesticides. In factories, antishrinking processes involve treatment with **chlorine**, which is then discharged to pollute waterways.

Always presoak and launder poly-cotton and synthetics before use, and steam clean wool carpets with plain water, to reduce pesticide residues. Whenever possible, choose such natural materials for your home as unbleached, untreated cotton for bed linen; pure cotton for covers and curtains; 100 percent wool for carpets and rugs. Clothing made from **organic** cotton is scarce but unbleached cotton clothing and underclothing is available. Organic cotton **bedding** for those suffering from allergies, is currently only available in the US. See also **Fabric dye**.

All fabrics are suitable for **recycling**. Dispose of unwanted items by giving them to charity shops, rummage sales, or rag merchants.

**Fabric
conditioner
Fabric dye
Fiberboard**

**Fabric conditioner** Fabric conditioners make **fabrics** feel softer but were also developed to reduce static electricity in synthetic materials. They are not necessary for natural fibers, especially those dried outside. If you prefer to use a fabric conditioner, choose **biodegradable** varieties that do not contain **detergent** or synthetic fragrance. You can also make your own from one part **bicarbonate of soda**, one part white **vinegar**, and two parts water. Scent it with two drops of **essential oil** of lemon, and use as you would a commercially-produced product.

**Fabric dye** Most commercial dyes are derived from **petro-chemicals**. **Chlorine** is also used in the dyeing process to achieve greater color fastness, as well as such hazardous **solvents** as **toluene**. **Sulphuric acid**, used to neutralize effluents from dye plants, further pollutes water that is already colored. This color cannot always be removed at sewage works and may then prevent light reaching plant life which dies, disrupting the food chain. Copper and chromium are among the metals used in dyeing that cause further pollution.

Try to avoid dark colors, especially reds. For nontoxic alternatives choose bedspreads, covers, and rugs that are neutral or light colors, or that are vegetable-dyed. Dobag rugs, for example, from northwestern Turkey, are made from pure wool that has been colored with traditional plant dyes. Look out also for hand-printed and vegetable-dyed Indian cotton bedspreads and rugs.

**Fiberboard** The two types of fiberboard commonly found in the home are hardboard and **medium density fiberboard (MDF)**. Hardboard has relatively low levels of resin binder, usually **formaldehyde**, while the manufacture of MDF uses higher levels to achieve greater strength. While fiberboard, especially MDF, is strong and durable, the formaldehyde binder emits toxic vapors that can irritate eyes, skin and lungs. Always seal fiberboard products with a nontoxic **paint** or **varnish**. A safer alternative material is a **sustainable softwood**. See also **Board**.

**Filler** The many types of filler on the market include **acrylic** and **cellulose** varieties, expanding filler, and two-part filler. Acrylic and cellulose fillers for cracks and small holes are safe to use, although it is wise to keep the uncured filler off your skin in case of sensitivity. Cellulose filler may irritate the eyes and lungs, so take precautions by wearing a dust mask if you are sanding down large areas, and keep it out of your eyes. Expanding filler is a foam containing **isocyanates**, toxic compounds that can cause severe lung irritation. Avoid it if you are asthmatic. Only use expanding filler in well-ventilated areas, and keep it off your skin. Two part wood filler consists of a resin and a hardener. The resin may contain the **solvent styrene**, and the active ingredient of the hardener, usually **benzoyl peroxide**, is an irritant. Wear gloves when using two-part fillers and keep them away from your eyes. If you are sanding them down, use a dust mask and be sure that the area is well ventilated.

**Filters** See **Air conditioning** and **Water filters**.

**Fir, Douglas** Grown in Western America, this **softwood** is a **sustainable timber**. See the list on p. 155.

**Fire extinguisher** Many fire extinguishers contain **halons**, some of which are thought to be even more destructive to the **ozone** layer than **CFCs**. Choose instead fire extinguishers that are labeled halon-free. These may use **carbon dioxide ($CO_2$)** to starve the fire of oxygen, or a powder. Keep them in the **kitchen** (p. 16) since this is the place where most accidents happen. To smother kitchen fires, started for example when hot fat ignites, the use of a fire blanket is recommended.

**Fire retardant** Most fire-retardant finishes are achieved using a **melamine formaldehyde** compound. All new furniture sold in the US is required by law to have either a spark-resistant cover, or a fire-retardant interlining fabric.

The regulations also cover mattresses and bed-base covers. If you are sensitive to formaldehyde, choose a mattress with a fire-retardant interlining and cover it with a fleece underblanket. Pure wool contains water and the protein keratin, making it slow to smolder and naturally flame-retardant. In the US, wool mattresses and futons are exempt from fire regulations. See also **Polyurethane foam**.

**Flameproof** See **Fire retardant**.

**Flea powder** The active ingredients of flea powders, sprays, collars, and shampoos for pets include **carbaryl, diazinon, dichlorvos**, and **lindane**. Dichlorvos, lindane, and carbaryl are suspected carcinogens, while diazinon is associated with reproductive problems. Cats are particularly susceptible to the harmful effects of dichlorvos and lindane, and dogs to carbaryl. These potent **insecticides** may also pose a health risk to young children who come into close contact with pets.

Discourage fleas by regularly brushing pets, and keep bedding and sleeping areas clean and aired. To get rid of flea larvae, thoroughly vacuum the house, and dispose of the dust bag by sealing it inside another bag. You can then sprinkle the dried flea-repelling herb, pennyroyal, in and around pets' bedding. Treat pets by rubbing an infusion of pennyroyal into their coats, or bathe them and rinse them well with the infusion. You can also buy concentrated pennyroyal oil, but do not use this on pregnant pets as, in rare cases, it has resulted in abortion. Other safe flea repellents include brewers' yeast sprinkled on your pets' food – one tablespoon a day for dogs, and one teaspoon for cats. You can also feed your pet one clove of garlic a day. Garlic discourages worms as well as fleas, but, like pennyroyal, it should not be given to pregnant pets.

**Flooring** Synthetic wall-to-wall **carpeting** has been treated with **formaldehyde**, a suspected carcinogen and a powerful irritant. Alternatives include pure **wool** carpets; plain, sanded **wood** floorboards treated with nontoxic **varnish**, plus **cotton** or wool rugs; natural **coir**, **seagrass**, and **sisal** matting for durability in hallways and **kitchen** (p.16); and **cork** and cork-based **linoleum**.

**Floor polish** See **Polish, floor and furniture**.

**Fluorescent lights** Pre-1978 fluorescent tubes have **ballasts**, starting devices, that contain toxic **PCBs (polychlorinated biphenyls)**. If the ballasts leak, air in the home can become contaminated. With older fluorescent lights, too, the flicker and hum may be noticeable and trigger such symptoms as irritability, eyestrain, and headaches. Modern fluorescents have been designed to reduce flickering and hum to an imperceptible level, so these should reduce symptoms. Fluorescents are also more **energy efficient** than incandescent lamps, and the new compact **low-energy bulbs** use 80 percent less electricity and last five times as long (8000 hours). See also **Lighting**, **Low-energy bulbs**.

**Fly killer** Solid-block fly killers and **aerosol** fly sprays often contain toxic **dichlorvos**, and some sprays contain **lindane**. Both these chemicals are suspected carcinogens and will contaminate the air you breathe, as well as any food that is left uncovered. Fly sprays containing **pyrethrins** are less hazardous, although some are powerful irritants. Fly papers are a safer alternative, and you can make your own by boiling equal parts of sugar, corn syrup and water together. Spread the mixture on strips cut from brown **paper** bags and hang them up. Another nontoxic alternative is to deter flies by keeping pots of such fly-repellent **herbs** as basil, rosemary, and thyme in the house, especially in the **kitchen** (p. 16); or place dried orange peel, lemon peel, and cloves in open jars.

**Foam packaging** Foamed **polystyrene** used for fresh produce, egg boxes, disposable cups, fast food, and protective **packaging** for fragile equipment, may still contain **ozone**-damaging **CFCs**. Some foam packaging, however, is CFC-free, while other types use a CFC with a lower ozone-depleting potential. Avoid over-packaged products and choose CFC-free **packaging**. Foam packaging is also difficult to **recycle**. When buying food, choose packaging that can be recycled or is made from recycled materials: a good example would be cardboard egg boxes.

**Formaldehyde** This colorless gas, also known as methanal, is normally used in solution. It is extensively used in industry as a resin binder and preservative, usually in **urea formaldehyde** or **melamine formaldehyde** compounds. Formaldehyde is used in all **board** products, such as **chip-**

Fluorescent
lights
Fly killer
Foam packaging
Formaldehyde

board; in **UFFI foam insulation** for cavity walls; as a finish for **"easy care"**, **"permanent press"**, **"non-iron"**, **fire-retardant** and synthetic **fabrics**; in finishes for synthetic **carpeting**; and in some shampoos. Formaldehyde gas can escape from all these sources and cause health problems: one US study concluded that one in five people can be sensitized by small amounts, and experience a powerful adverse reaction to formaldehyde whenever they encounter it. Formaldehyde is a suspected carcinogen and a potent irritant that affects the eyes and lungs, and can cause dizziness and headaches.

Avoid products containing formaldehyde. Be sure all types of board are sealed with **paint** or a nontoxic **varnish**, and thoroughly launder any synthetic or natural/synthetic blend fabrics before use to reduce any excess formaldehyde concentrations that have built up in the packaging. Choose natural materials and fabrics for your home and see **Board**, **Bedding**, **Fabric** for safe alternatives.

**Formic acid**
**Fossil fuels**
**Freezer**

**Formic acid** This strong-smelling acid is an ingredient of some types of **descaler** for kettles. It is hazardous if inhaled and is also a skin irritant. Guard against accidentally splashing your skin or eyes with products containing formic acid, and make sure there is adequate **ventilation**. See **Descaler** for safe alternatives.

**Fossil fuels** The burning of fossil fuels – **coal**, oil, and **gas** – for heat and power, has made the most significant contribution to one of our major global environmental problems, the **greenhouse effect**. Supplies of fossil fuels are also dwindling and extraction is becoming increasingly expensive. A positive step you can take as a householder to slow down and stabilize both consumption of fossil fuels and the greenhouse effect is **energy saving**.

**Freezer** After an electric **stove**, an electric freezer is the most costly appliance to run. Chest freezers are more efficient than upright models since cold air sinks and you lose less when you open the lid. Siting them in an unheated **garage** (p. 48), porch, or **basement** (p. 50) will reduce running costs. If you are thinking of buying a freezer, consider whether a **refrigerator-freezer** would satisfy your requirements. A full freezer is more **energy efficient** than an empty one: it takes more energy to chill empty space.

Choose models with reduced **CFC** levels that have low wattages, and remember to defrost regularly.

**Full-spectrum lighting** Natural light is essential for good health and for the production of vitamin D. During the winter months, however, and in many homes and workplaces, we rely on **artificial light**. Sensitive people may develop such symptoms – collectively known as SAD syndrome – as depression, weight gain, and lethargy, in response to inadequate supplies of daylight. One solution is to try full-spectrum bulbs, available for incandescent or fluorescent fixtures. These give out slightly higher levels of UV than standard bulbs, and the light given off closely replicates the spectrum of daylight. Full-spectrum lighting, however, should only be used on a small scale, and not as a replacement for standard lighting. In some instances high UV levels may react adversely with airborne pollutants, resulting in photochemical smog.

**Fungicides** These chemicals destroy or prevent the growth of fungus and **mold**. They are commonly found in such products as **paint**, **timber treatments**, **wood preservative**, tile **adhesives**, **grout**, and **wallpaper paste**. Fungicides are irritants so keep them off your skin and protect your eyes when using products that contain them.

**Furnace** A forced-air **gas** or oil furnace may be wasting considerable **energy** unless it's of a modern, **energy-efficient** "pulse" design. These newer pulse furnaces use advanced combustion techniques, sometimes in combination with a **heat exchanger**, to increase thermal efficiency, from around 60 percent to as high as 85 or 90 percent, thus saving on fuel and reducing the amount of harmful pollutants in the flue gas. See also **Central heating**, **Energy**.

**Furniture** Avoid furniture and millwork made from **tropical hardwoods**. These come from the rainforests, and widespread depletion of this resource is one of the major causes of the **greenhouse effect**. Choose instead furniture made from such fast-growing **softwoods** as **pine** and **spruce**; from such temperate **hardwoods** as **ash**, **beech** or **oak**; look for **hardwoods** from managed plantations; and consider buying second-hand furniture. See the list of **sustainable timber** on p. 155. ▷

Upholstered furniture made since 1950 may contain **polyurethane foam**, a serious fire hazard. Once alight, the foam burns rapidly to give off dense smoke and toxic fumes. New upholstered furniture must, by law, contain safer, combustion-modified foam that slows down the spread of fire. Furniture made before 1950 is exempt from regulations since polyurethane foam was not invented until after that date.

**Furniture polish** See **Polish, floor and furniture**.

**Futon** Traditional Japanese futons are slim mattresses filled with **wool** or natural fibers. They may be placed directly on the floor and can be rolled up during the day for extra space. Choose futon bases made from solid **softwoods**.

**Furniture polish**
**Futon**

**Gaboon** This endangered **tropical hardwood** is also known as **okoume**. Avoid products made from gaboon and see the list of **sustainable timber** on p. 155 for alternatives.

**Gaia house** A house designed according to the principles of health, ecology, and spiritual harmony.

**Gamma-HCH** See **Lindane**.

**Gas** Natural gas, composed mainly of **methane**, is over 30 percent more **energy efficient** than electricity when burnt. Gas production is also less polluting than electricity production by coal-fired power stations since it creates 40 percent less **carbon dioxide**, the main contributor to the **greenhouse effect**. Due to its instant heat control, a gas **stove** is less expensive to run than an electric model. If you are installing gas **central heating**, the most efficient boiler you can buy is a **gas-condensing boiler**; high-efficiency pulse **furnaces** are also available. When choosing new appliances for your home, consider changing to gas. Natural gas escaping from gasfields, mains, and appliances, however, could be a problem since methane is a greenhouse gas that is 20 times more potent than $CO_2$.

**Gas-condensing boiler** This is the most efficient type of **boiler** you can use in your home if you have a hydronic heating system. **Gas** is less environmentally polluting than electricity and is a more cost-efficient fuel. The condensing boiler uses a second or a larger **heat exchanger** to extract additional **energy** from the flue gases that a standard boiler allows to escape, thus achieving up to 20 percent greater efficiency. Although initially more expensive than standard boilers, the increased efficiency of the gas-condensing boiler will be reflected in lower fuel bills, with savings of up to 15 percent annually. The condensing action of this type of boiler also prevents acidic water vapor escaping to fall later as acid rain.

**Gasoline**
**Glass**

**Gasoline** Obtained by distillation of **petroleum** in oil refineries, gasoline is a complex mixture of **hydrocarbons**, including toxic **benzene**, plus such additives as antiknock compounds, detergents, and dispersants. Leaded gasoline is no longer available in the US, since tetraethyl **lead** has been linked to impaired mental development of children, and to damage to the nervous system, kidneys, and reproductive system of adults. The fumes given off by gasoline are particularly harmful. While you are filling up your **car** at a gas pump, benzene evaporates from the pump hose and escapes into the air. In California special extractor pumps at filling stations prevent the benzene vapors from escaping. Benzene in high doses is a carcinogen, while repeated low doses cause such symptoms as dizziness, headaches, and bleeding gums. When gasoline is burned, harmful **exhaust gases** pollute the air, contribute to the **greenhouse effect**, and react with sunlight to form a photo chemical smog.

Keep all gasoline and related products off your skin. If you drive a car more than 15 years old, consider updating to one fitted with a three-way **catalytic converter**. This device will reduce the emission of pollutant gases by around 90 percent. When filling up your fuel tank, try not to inhale the fumes; stand as far back from the opening to the gasoline tank as you can.

**Glass** Manufacturing glass is an **energy**-intensive process, and quarrying the raw materials – sand, limestone, and soda ash – can disfigure the environment. Glass, however, can be recycled over and over again with no appreciable reduction in quality. **Recycling** glass conserves both fuel and natural resources. For each ton of broken glass (cullet) used, 32 gallons of oil are saved, plus 1.2 tons of raw materials. In the US, estimates show that around 28 billion glass **bottles** and jars are used annually. Of this total, only about 11 percent are recycled and reused. Always return returnable bottles. Take used bottles and jars to your local **bottle bank**, or reclamation center, and look for drinking glasses, dishes, and jugs made from tough, recycled glass when shopping. See also **Recycling**.

**Global warming** See **Greenhouse effect**.

**Gloss paint** Gloss paint is mostly produced from such non-renewable resources as oil, and contains higher levels of **solvents** than **emulsion paint**. **Polyurethane** and **silicone** may be added for extra durability and improved water-repellent properties. Until recently **lead** was an ingredient of gloss paint, but now most commercial brands have no added lead. The vapors from such solvents as **xylene** in gloss paint may be toxic, so be sure that the area you are working in is well ventilated. Gloss paint is also flammable. See **Paint, organic** for safe alternatives.

**Granite** In many of the granite areas of the US, and other geological areas as well, hazardous **radon** gas can seep into homes from the subsoil via cracks, and also through the **water** supply. Inhaling radon gas can seriously damage lung tissue. See **Radon**.

**Greenhouse effect** The composition of the gases in the atmosphere keeps our planet at a habitable temperature by a natural process – the greenhouse effect. Radiation from the sun passes through the atmosphere and warms the surface of the planet. The Earth, in turn, re-radiates the energy in a changed form, called infrared heat. Some atmospheric gases, like **carbon dioxide ($CO_2$)**, absorb this infrared heat and so the atmosphere is warmed, and hence the Earth is kept warmer than it would otherwise be. Since the Industrial Revolution, however, we have added about 25 percent more $CO_2$ plus significant quantities of other "greenhouse gases" and chemicals to the atmosphere. This has resulted in a change to the protective layer which, as a direct consequence, traps more heat that warms the Earth. In the last hundred years the Earth's temperature has risen by $1^\circ F$ and the 1980s saw four of the hottest years on record. Latest estimates predict an increase in global temperature of between 2.7 and 8.1°F by the year 2040. Such an increase brings a real danger of massive disruption to global weather patterns, resulting in extreme conditions, such as hurricanes, and flooding of the low-lying land areas where 40 percent of the world's population currently lives. The other main greenhouse gases are **CFCs**, **methane**, **nitrogen oxides**, and also tropospheric **ozone**, created when sunlight reacts with atmospheric pollutants. Cutting down and burning large areas of rainforest for grazing and agriculture, and the commercial logging of **tropical hardwood**, releases at least 2.2 billion tons of $CO_2$ into the atmosphere per annum.

Current thinking by scientists sees **energy** efficiency by industry and the consumer alike, as the most hopeful method of slowing down the rise in global temperature. See **Energy**, **Energy efficient**, **Energy saving**.

**Grout**
**Gypsum**
**Hair-care products**
**Halogen lamps**

**Grout** Grout, a thin, coarse mortar, is used for filling the spaces between tiles and comes in two types: **cement**-based and epoxy grout. Cement-based grout is an irritant and prolonged contact can cause skin burns. The epoxy type is milder but may also irritate sensitive skins. Grout may contain **fungicides**, also skin irritants, so take precautions by wearing gloves and keeping grout off your skin. Both types of grout are nontoxic when set.

**Gypsum** A naturally occurring mineral, gypsum is made into **plaster** and plasterboard for interior plastering and finishing. Gypsum is a natural, nontoxic material but the dust may be irritating. Wear a dust mask when mixing plaster. Avoid products made from phosphogypsum as these may contain **radon**.

**Hair-care products** See **Toiletries**.

**Halogen lamps** Tungsten-halogen lamps are a type of **incandescent lamp** with miniature bulbs made from quartz glass. The powerful white light they give out is close to daylight in quality. Although initially expensive, tungsten-halogen bulbs can provide up to 4000 hours of use. Halogen bulbs do, however, emit ultraviolet radiation (UVR). In September 1990, out of eight tungsten-halogen desk lamps tested by the UK Consumers' Association, seven gave out UVR levels that exceeded international safety limits, and UVR exposure is linked to skin cancer. Some of the lamps tested have now been withdrawn from sale. If you already have, or are considering buying, a tungsten-halogen desk lamp, ask for specifications to ascertain its UVR output. Use this type of lamp with care: follow the safety advice on the instructions, and choose the low output setting if this is available. Halogen bulbs are also used in projectors and some **stove** eyes. UVR emissions from such appliances are not thought to be harmful since the bulbs are usually covered with a filter, and exposure to light from these sources is not normally extensive. See also **Lighting**.

**Halons** Propellant gases found in some types of **fire extinguisher**, halons are similar in composition to **CFCs**. The bromine they contain (except for Halon 14) destroys **ozone molecules**. Choose halon-free extinguishers.

**Hardwoods** This term distinguishes the wood of non-coniferous, broadleafed trees such as **oak** and **ash**, from **softwood**. It refers to the cell-structure of the timber, and is an important distinction in the timber trade. Most **tropical hardwood** is from rainforests. Buying such tropical hardwood as **teak**, **mahogany**, and **ramin** from unsustainable sources contributes to the **greenhouse effect**, the displacement of indigenous peoples, and the loss of valuable medicinal plant species. Although tropical hardwood may be appropriate for structural and external building applications, it is not necessary for interior use. Choose hardwoods only from sustainable sources: these include such temperate hardwoods as oak from North America, or **beech**. Another option is to select a softwood such as **pine** that is specifically grown for furniture and joinery. See also **Softwoods**, and the list of **sustainable timber** on p. 155 for other alternatives.

**Hazardous waste** In the US and most industrialized European countries, it is unlawful to dump hazardous **waste** into domestic waste sites. In the US, there are hundreds of hazardous waste sites in operation, but toxic waste continues to find its way into domestic landfill sites. This practice is known as "co-disposal". Over one-half of the US population gets its **drinking water** from underground sources. Leakage from both toxic and domestic sites is widespread, allowing carcinogenic chemicals and such toxic heavy metals as **cadmium** to work their way slowly into groundwater supplies and contaminate drinking water.

Most toxic waste in the US originates from industry, but domestic waste also generates poisons that threaten to contaminate water supplies. To reduce your own contribution, the first step is to use nontoxic products whenever possible. Then, if you do need to dispose of toxic waste, contact your local health authority or the Environmental Protection Agency (EPA) for details of the hazardous waste disposal pickup in your region. If facilities are not available, contact a commercial handler and arrange a bulk collection with friends and neighbors. You can also contact environmental organizations for advice.

**HDPE plastic**
**Heat exchanger**

### To minimize the risks from household waste

- Buy natural, nontoxic household products whenever possible, and choose those with **packaging** that is **biodegradable**. Choose products with minimum packaging and buy in bulk whenever you can.

- Do not throw away partially-used **aerosols**: they explode when incinerated, discharging polluting gases into the air.

- Do not dispose of **batteries**, **gloss paint**, **paint stripper**, **paint thinner**, **white spirit**, **metal**, **polish**, wood stain, or **wood preservative** with household waste. Seal tightly and store for disposal as hazardous waste.

- Do not pour **gasoline**, **engine oil**, **brake and clutch fluid** down the drain to contaminate water supplies. Take them to a service station or local reclamation center for **recycling** or disposal.

**HDPE plastic** See **Plastic**.

**Heat exchanger** This **energy-saving** device, also known as a "heat recovery ventilator", recycles domestic heat. A heat exchanger is also used in some domestic appliances, for example in a **refrigerator** and a **boiler** to improve efficiency. A **gas-condensing boiler** uses an additional or a larger heat exchanger. Heat exchangers work by transferring heat from the warm, stale airstream leaving the room to the cooler, incoming stream of fresher air. Heat exchangers work well in combination with **solar-heating** methods.

Solar **energy** absorbed by a conservatory or greenhouse, for example, can be transferred indoors via a heat and recovery ventilator.

**Heat gun** To remove **paint**, a heat gun is a safe alternative to toxic **paint stripper**. It is also preferable to a **propane torch** that will vaporize **lead** particles from old paint, and scorch wood. The safest combination for stripping paint is a heat gun plus a scraper, or a nontoxic paint stripper.

**Heating** An average **central-heating** system uses 14,000 kWh of electricity a year, producing 15.4 tons of **carbon dioxide ($CO_2$)**, the major greenhouse gas, plus 370 pounds of polluting **sulphur dioxide** and 108 pounds of **nitrogen oxides**. Sulphur dioxides and nitrogen oxides are atmospheric pollutants that combine to form **acid rain**. It has been estimated that electricity creates 73 percent of the acid rain produced in the UK. **Coal** fired power stations are also inefficient. They operate at around 35 percent efficiency with the rest lost as steam. Efficiency also decreases as electricity travels through the cables of the power grid. **Gas**, on the other hand creates 40 percent less carbon dioxide than electricity and gas-fired central heating is 30 percent more efficient than electric. A **gas-condensing boiler** is 20 percent more efficient than standard boilers. The condensing action also prevents acidic water vapor from escaping to fall later as acid rain. Wood-burning stoves are available that use catalytic combustion for maximum energy and minimum emissions of **combustion gases**. Oil and this type of solid fuel heating produce around half the pollution of electricity, and solid fuel is about 70 percent efficient. Open fires are the least efficient form of heating: 80 percent of the heat is lost up the chimney. See **Central heating, Energy**.

**Heat pump** A heat pump is a convenient, yet not particularly efficient, **central heating** and cooling appliance designed around a refrigeration-type compressor. Inexpensive to install, it is, unfortunately, not so economical to operate, especially in colder climates. The benefit of a heat pump is that it serves as both a heating and an **air-conditioning** system, drawing heat from inside the house on warm days, and extracting heat from outside on days that are cooler. On particularly cold days, the system

Heat gun
Heating
Heat pump

needs supplemental heat from an auxiliary burner or electrical element to provide warmth, which increases operating costs and increases dependence on coal-fired electrical **energy**, which adds to **acid rain** and the **greenhouse effect**. See also **Central heating**, **Energy**, and **Air conditioning**.

**Hemlock, Western** This North American tree is a **softwood** that is used for construction and general joinery. It is included in the list of **sustainable timber** on p. 155.

**Herbs** Herbs are highly versatile plants that have a wide variety of uses in the home. Both fresh and dried herbs are healthy additions to the diet. Herbs can also act as **insect repellents**. The **essential oil** from plants, too, can act as a **disinfectant**, a relaxant, and an **air freshener**. Bowls of herbal **pot-pourri** will sweeten indoor air, and if you have trouble sleeping, try using a **hop pillow**. Choose natural, **biodegradable** household cleaners that are often plant-based. Natural **paint** also uses plant oils and resins. Herbal **toiletries** are gentler for skin and hair, and are usually **cruelty-free** products. Many herbal toiletries are also biodegradable. Herbal preparations are less harmful to children than prescribed drugs if accidentally swallowed. The ingredients are generally from renewable resources and the manufacturing process does not entail the kind of chemical pollution discharged into the environment from pharmaceutical factories.

**Hickory** A **hardwood** grown in North America, this produces tough, **sustainable timber**. See the list on p. 155.

**Hop pillow** If you are not sleeping well, try using a pillow stuffed with hops. Hops contain a sedative called lupulin that helps many people to improve their sleeping patterns. You can buy hop pillows from health stores, or make your own. Make a bag from muslin to fit inside a small pillowcase. Fill it with dried hops, close the open end, insert it into the case, and put it beside your pillow.

**Horsehair** Antique furniture is often stuffed with horsehair. Although most furniture now uses **polyurethane foam**, horsehair is however still used in such items as **mattresses**, and in traditional upholstery. It may cause allergic reactions in some people.

**Hot-air treatment** This is a non-chemical, remedial **timber treatment** for rot and beetle attacks. Used in historic buildings in the UK, treatment involves drying out the timber with hot air and plenty of **ventilation** while special equipment carefully monitors and controls temperature and humidity. At present, however, companies carrying out this treatment will not give a standard 30-year guarantee. See also **Timber treatments**.

**House plants** All plants take in **carbon dioxide** and give out oxygen during sunlight hours, helping to freshen air. House plants are not only decorative, they purify and filter indoor air by absorbing a variety of pollutants from **tobacco smoke** to **formaldehyde**. Microorganisms present in the plant soil also clean the air, trapping such gases as **carbon monoxide**. Some rooms in the home may have poor air quality due to fumes from heating appliances and formaldehyde vapors from **chipboard**. Four or five plants in such rooms will significantly improve indoor air. Be sure to include spider plants, *Chlorophytum elatum* var. *vittatum,* as they are efficient absorbers of formaldehyde and tobacco smoke. Scented plants, for example, lemon geraniums, are a good choice for **kitchens** (p. 16), and pots of such **herbs** as basil will repel flies as well as flavor dishes. Ferns profit from moisture so they are a good choice for **bathrooms** (p. 80). All plants will improve the air you breathe. Arrange them in groups so they can more easily maintain the levels of humidity they need, especially in drier, centrally-heated rooms.

**Humidifier** Dry, indoor air may irritate the nose and throat. One solution is to invest in a humidifier. This device will replace lost moisture, but may become a health hazard if the water reservoir inside is not thoroughly cleaned and disinfected. Humidifiers, like **air-conditioning systems**, are particularly prone to contamination by bacteria, fungi, and **molds**. When these are released into the air, such symptoms as runny noses, breathing problems, and headaches can result. A cheaper and non-mechanical way to humidify indoor air is to install permanent vents in **windows**, open windows, or place bowls of water near radiators. Put a few drops of **essential oil** into the water to add fragrance and freshen air.

A bathroom with toilet consumes between 60 and 70 percent of your daily domestic water supply. As well as being wasteful, this "healthy" part of the house may also contain products employing a variety of strong and potentially harmful chemicals.

**Bathroom fixtures** An average bath uses considerably more water than a **shower**. Take a short shower instead of bathing, and consider installing a shower with a low-flow head; this uses about half as much water as a standard nozzle. A standard **toilet** can use up to 3.4 gallons per flush. To reduce the amount used, place **bottles** filled with water in the cistern, making sure they are well clear of the flushing mechanism. Consider installing a **dual-flush** or **low-flush** toilet that uses about half as much water per flush as a standard model.

**Bathroom cleaners Bleach** or bleach-based cleaners contain such **chlorine**-derived compounds as **sodium hypochlorite**. The fumes given off by this chemical are toxic. NEVER mix chlorine-based bleach with cleaners containing **ammonia**: the resulting chlorine gas can prove fatal if inhaled. Chlorine-free bleaches based on **hydrogen peroxide** or **sodium percarbonate** are much safer. If you have a septic tank, do not use bleach at all, since it destroys the beneficial bacteria in the tank. **Biodegradable** toilet cleaners that do not

damage septic tanks are now available. However, these contain **acetic acid**. **Descaler** products for removing limescale may contain **phosphoric acid**, which if splashed into the eyes or on to the skin, can cause serious burns. An effective home-made descaler consists of powdered **citric acid** or lemon juice. **Borax** is another nontoxic product with descaling properties, as is plain white **vinegar**. Vinegar is also an effective disinfectant, that works without polluting the water supply. **Toilet freshener block** usually contains the toxic chemical **para-dichlorobenzene**. A safer alternative is to put a few drops of an antiseptic **essential oil**, such as lemon, lavender, or pine, into the

1 Window for ventilation and light
2 Pot-pourri
3 Tiles
4 Low-flow shower head
5 Enclosed lights
6 Cotton rug
7 Lockable medicine cabinet
8 Cruelty-free, herbal toiletries
9 Essential oils
10 Nontoxic bathroom cleaners
11 Organic paint
12 House plants
13 Dual-flush toilet
14 Recycled or unbleached toilet paper

toilet bowl. Other options include keeping a scented plant or a bowl of **pot-pourri** next to the toilet, opening a window, or installing a permanent vent. These measures are also good alternatives to **air freshener**.

**Medicine cabinet** Prescribed drugs are often powerful chemicals that must be kept locked away from children. Return old medicines or drugs to your doctor or pharmacist for disposal.

**Condensation, moisture, and mold** These problems can be avoided if there is adequate **ventilation** in the bathroom. Avoid using wallpaper or **paint** made of **vinyl**. It is an impermeable material and will trap moisture behind it. Use materials that "breathe", such as **cork**, or paint walls with emulsion or **organic paint**. Use tiles in areas liable to splashing and wipe walls and shower curtains after use to inhibit mold. If mold is already present, clean with vinegar and water or a borax solution. Borax helps to deter mold.

**Radon** If you live in a high-risk area, this radioactive gas can enter your water supply. It is then dispersed and inhaled in the form of hot steam from the shower or bath. Be sure the bathroom is well ventilated. Contact your local environmental health office to get radon levels checked and seek advice on precautionary steps.

**Hydrocarbons** This large class of chemicals covers a range of compounds that contain only carbon and hydrogen, but in varying proportions and structures. Many hydrocarbons are used as fuels and **solvents**. **Gasoline** is a blend of highly flammable hydrocarbons, which cause drowsiness if inhaled. Hazardous hydrocarbons commonly found in solvents are **toluene** and **xylene**. All hydrocarbons are flammable, some are suspected carcinogens, and many are toxic. A link has been suggested between pregnant women's exposure to hydrocarbons and an increased risk of birth defects. Hydrocarbons also provoke allergic reactions in sensitive people. See under individual hydrocarbon entries for more information on these chemicals.

**Hydrocarbons
Hydrogen
peroxide**

**Hydrogen peroxide** Also called **oxygen bleach**, and commonly used as a **bleach**, a mild **disinfectant**, and mouthwash, hydrogen peroxide is toxic if swallowed in sufficient quantities. In low concentrations, such as those used for lightening hair, it may irritate the skin. Highly-concentrated solutions are employed for bleaching **wood**, and these can cause burns. Hydrogen peroxide rapidly decomposes, even explosively, especially with warmth and sunlight, which is why it is sold in dark bottles. Many companies are now switching from **chlorine bleach** to hydrogen peroxide bleach, because it breaks down so readily and is less harmful to the **water** supply.

**Incandescent lamps** See **Lighting** and **Low-energy bulbs**.

**Insecticides** These substances are designed to kill such insects as ants, aphids, flies, fleas, and wasps. The active ingredient of many insecticides is a powerful and toxic chemical that may pollute indoor air, provoke allergic reactions, and harm household pets. Commonly used insecticides include **diazinon** and **dichlorvos**. See under individual entries.

**Insect repellent** The common active ingredient of insect repellents is **diethyl toluamide (DEET)**, which is used in gels and sprays to repel flies, gnats, and mosquitoes. Repeated exposure to DEET has resulted in damage to the brain and nervous system in some cases, while serious skin problems have also been caused by applying strong solutions of DEET. Do not use insect repellents on a regular basis, and avoid using them on small children. A safe and effective repellent for gnats and mosquitoes is to rub **vinegar** on the skin. Other herbal alternatives, with a more pleasant scent, include **essential oil** of citronella or lavender: dilute a few drops in a little vegetable oil and rub on. Growing such **herbs** as basil in the home is also said to deter flying insects from coming inside.

**Insulation** As much as half the heat generated in an average house may be lost through inadequate insulation and leaky roof, walls, and **windows**. Heat also escapes through gaps in baseboards, floorboards, and above and below doors. Upgrading home insulation is an **energy-saving** measure that could reduce fuel bills by up to 25 percent and make your house more comfortable. Conserving **energy** also lessens the load on the environment since less demand for energy means reduced consumption of natural resources and less pollution. Begin by carrying out simple and inexpensive insulation measures on your home and progress to larger improvements. **Double glazing** is not recommended on economic grounds alone unless you are having new windows installed; the expense of going to double glazing takes many years to recoup.

### Low-cost measures

**Insulation (continued)**

- Use **weatherstripping** on doors and windows, around the attic hatch, and also around pipes where they pass through the ceiling. Seal gaps between floorboards, and between floor and baseboards.
- Insulate your water heater with a good-quality cylinder jacket. If the existing jacket is worn, put another over the top.
- Hang heavy, lined curtains and draw them at dusk. Make sure that they do not overhang radiators that are situated under windows or heat will escape up behind them.
- If you have radiators against outside walls, place a sheet of reflective foil behind them (shiny side out) to reflect heat back into the room.
- Lay felt under your carpet to keep in more heat.
- If you have open fireplaces, install draft-proof covers when they are not in use.

### Larger-scale improvements

- Insulate your attic with at least 4 inches, but preferably, 6 inches of insulation. Avoid extruded **polystyrene**, which contains **CFCs** and choose **cellulose** fiber, or **vermiculite** chips. As the attic will be colder after insulation, you will also need to wrap pipes and tanks to prevent freezing. See also **Insulation materials**.

When insulating your home, however, remember to retain adequate **ventilation**. Air pollution can build up inside an overly-sealed home, so good ventilation is essential, especially in rooms with fuel-burning heaters. This type of heater can emit such hazardous **combustion gases** as **carbon monoxide**.

**Insulation materials** Extruded **polystyrene** insulation contains ozone-damaging **CFCs**. Avoid this product and choose instead **cellulose fiber** or **vermiculite** chips. For walls and floors, you can also use natural **cork**. Mineral wool is another alternative but studies have implicated mineral fibers as a cause of lung cancer. Vermiculite chips may be a safer option – they are non-irritant and contain no synthetic chemicals. Avoid **UFFI foam** cavity-wall insulation. In many countries this foam is considered a health risk and has been banned. It contains high levels of **urea formaldehyde** resin that continue to release **formaldehyde** gas into rooms long after the initial installation. Formaldehyde is a suspected carcinogen

**Ionizer** All mechanical and electrical equipment, especially the **TV** and **VDT**, and synthetic materials that produce static, increase the positive ions in the atmosphere and deplete the level of the beneficial negative ions. Negative ions are associated with feelings of well-being and are found in abundance in seaside or mountain air. Conversely, air that is charged with positive ions, as, for example, before a storm, can make you feel stressful and heavy. An ionizer will replace negative ions and is said to improve concentration and increase vitality. Try an ionizer if you work for long periods in front of a VDT: ionizers are silent and inexpensive to run.

**Iroko** This is a **tropical hardwood** and an endangered **timber**. Avoid products made from this wood unless supplies are from managed plantations. See **Softwoods** for alternatives and **sustainable timber** list on p. 155.

**Iron** A metal that occurs naturally in **water** supplies in some areas, iron can corrode water pipes and discolor your tap water. Iron should not make water unsafe to drink, but if you are concerned, a **water filter** will reduce levels of this metal.

**Isocyanates** These compounds are used in the manufacture of two-part resin **adhesives**. Isocyanates can irritate the

skin and sensitive people may experience severe respiratory problems after exposure to small quantities. Do not breathe in the vapor of two-part resins, and keep them off your skin. See **Adhesives** for safer alternatives.

**Isopropanol** Isopropanol, or isopropyl alcohol, is a **solvent** found in some **de-icers** and computer disk-drive cleaners. Isopropanol is irritating to the eyes and highly flammable. Keep it off your skin and, in particular, guard against splashing your eyes. As a general rule, do not inhale solvent vapors.

**Jacaranda** See **Rosewood**.

**Jelutong** This is a **tropical hardwood** and classified as an endangered **timber**. Unless it can be demonstrated that the timber comes from managed plantations, avoid products made from jelutong. See the list of **sustainable timber** on p. 155 for alternatives.

**Jute** The stems of the jute plant are processed with hemp to make hessian (burlap) for wall coverings, sacking, and backing for **linoleum**.

**Kapok** The tropical silk-cotton tree produces kapok fibers which are used to fill cushions, some bedding, and quilted clothing. Kapok makes a natural, soft, and light stuffing but will break down and release dust after prolonged wear. Replace the stuffing periodically and beware of the dust if you suffer from allergies.

**Kapur** Avoid this endangered **tropical hardwood** unless supplies come from managed plantations. See the list of **sustainable timber** on p. 155 for alternatives.

**Kempas** This **tropical hardwood** is an endangered **timber**. Avoid products made from kempas unless the timber comes from managed plantations. See the list of **sustainable timber** on p. 155 for alternatives.

**Kerosene** A **hydrocarbon** used for space heating and cooking. Kerosene fumes may be harmful if inhaled and spilling the liquid on your skin can cause rashes. When burned, kerosene gives off such pollutants as **sulphur**

Isopropanol
Jacaranda
Jelutong
Jute
Kapok
Kapur
Kempas
Kerosene

**dioxide**, so always open windows in rooms where kerosene heaters are used. Poor ventilation with this type of heating can lead to **condensation**.

**Keruing** This endangered species is a **tropical hardwood** that is to be avoided unless the **timber** comes from managed plantations. See the list of **sustainable timber** on p. 155 for alternatives.

**Kettle** Heat only as much **water** as you need at a time. Turn the kettle off as soon as it boils, or invest in an electric model with an automatic cut-off switch. Coffee-makers, too, can use more **energy** than you might realize, especially the auto-drip variety. Jug-type kettles make it possible to boil small amounts of water but they tend to be made of **plastic**: tiny plastic particles will eventually dissolve into your water. In view of the possible link between **aluminum** and Alzheimer's disease, it may be wise to avoid aluminum kettles too. Choose stainless steel, and ensure that your kettle is free from scale by using a nontoxic commercial **descaler** or **vinegar**. Scale-coated kettles use more **energy**. Filling your kettle from a **water filter** helps prevent scale deposits.

Keruing
Kettle
Kitchen
appliances
Kitchen foil

**Kitchen appliances** Many of the increasing numbers of appliances used in the modern **kitchen** (p. 16) waste valuable **energy** and **water**. Before buying any new appliance for your kitchen, consider whether it is really necessary. If it is, study test reports such as those published by Consumers' Associations and compare different models to be sure that you choose the most **energy-efficient** appliance. When buying a **refrigerator**, **freezer**, or refrigerator-freezer, choose models that use insulating foam with reduced **CFC** levels. See individual appliance entries for **Dishwasher, Freezer, Kettle, Microwave, Refrigerator, Stove**, and **Washing machine.**

**Kitchen foil** See **Aluminum foil**.

**Larch**
**Latex**
**Lauan**
**Laundry powder**

**Larch** A native European **hardwood**. Larch is a **sustainable timber** that is used for planking and heavy construction. See the list of sustainable timber on p. 155.

**Latex** This milky fluid from **rubber** trees is a versatile, natural substance that can be processed into foam for mattresses. Latex foam contains tiny air holes that keep mattresses well ventilated. The absence of feathers, dust, or fluff makes them particularly suitable for people with allergies, especially asthma.

**Lauan** Supplies of this **tropical hardwood**, imported mainly from the Philippines, are scarce because sustainable management of forests is not possible. Avoid products made from lauan unless it can be demonstrated that the **timber** comes from managed plantations. Choose instead products made from a **sustainable timber**, listed on p. 155.

**Laundry powder** Brands of laundry powder, or **detergent**, currently available contain most of the following ingredients: **bleach**, **enzymes**, **optical brighteners**, **phosphates**, **surfactants**, and synthetic fragrance. Surfactants clean your washing, separating and removing the dirt, and most surfactants are based on **petrochemicals**. Phosphates soften the **water** and enhance the cleaning power of the surfactants. They are not, however, **biodegradable** and, since few sewage plants are equipped to remove them, phosphates persist in waterways. In slow-moving rivers and lakes, phosphates are responsible for eutrophication the clogging of the water's surface by tiny green algae that results in the suffocation of fish, as well as plants beneath the surface. Optical brighteners make your washing appear whiter by giving off a fluorescent bluish white light. They do not make your wash any cleaner. Enzymes, an ingredient of **biological** laundry powders, break down such proteins as blood and milk, and improve stain-removing capability. Bleach, usually **sodium perborate**, not **chlorine bleach**, is added for stain removal but is not activated until the water reaches a high temperature. The bleach stabilizer, **EDTA**, is often added and can pose problems, as it absorbs heavy metals from river beds and reintroduces them into the environment.

**Laundry powder (continued)**

The issue that has given most cause for concern is the environmental acceptability of laundry powders, mainly due to the level of phosphates they contain. Stretches of water in parts of the US have already been damaged by eutrophication and are still clogged and lifeless. In Switzerland, phosphates have been banned but **NTA**, the substitute used, causes similar pollution problems to EDTA. Phosphate-free washing powders are now available that use **zeolites**, crystalline substances that are not considered to be harmful to the environment. Brands that are phosphate-free may still contain bleach, enzymes and optical brighteners although most do not contain the stabilizer, EDTA. If you want to avoid bleach altogether, choose a liquid detergent, as these contain no bleach, or try one of the few bleach-free powders. Enzymes have been linked to skin problems in sensitive people who may also be allergic to the fragrance. If you have sensitive skin, or suffer from eczema, choose non-biological powders or liquids, as these are less likely to irritate.

Although phosphate-free brands tend to be more expensive to buy, you need less of them, so they can work out cheaper. From the environmental point of view, phosphate-free powders are more acceptable since they do not add to the problem of water pollution and help reduce the phosphate level in rivers. Phosphate-free liquid detergents are also available and these are recommended for sensitive skins. They are, however, more expensive than powders and less efficient at removing stains. Liquid varieties that can be added to a plastic ball dispenser and put straight in the drum are more economical, since powder from the dispenser is often wasted by falling directly through the drum before the machine has filled. Do not use too much powder: most manufacturers recommend the use of more powder than necessary.

**Lead** This heavy metal has a wide variety of uses from piping, roofing, and soldering **cans**, to an additive for **gasoline**, and a lubricant for engine valves when in a modified form. Lead and lead compounds are highly toxic. It can damage children's health and mental abilities as well as affect the reproductive system. It can also harm the kidneys and the nervous system, and damage muscles. Lead does not biodegrade; it accumulates in the atmosphere or soil where it remains forever. Until very recently, the major threat of lead poisoning came from car emissions. However, since the introduction of unleaded gasoline this threat is slowly diminishing, and since 1975 all new cars sold in the US were required by law to be capable of running on unleaded fuel. If your car still runs only on leaded fuel, consult your dealer; it will likely take unleaded gas without causing any damage.

**Lead**
**Light bulbs**

Today, the other major source of lead poisoning in the home remains the **water** supply, and a recent government report has recommended a drastic reduction in the current safety limits set for lead in **drinking water**. It has been estimated that as much as a third of all lead intake may still be due to water supplied through lead or lead-soldered pipes to homes and older institutional buildings. Buildings may have lead piping either inside, or outside where pipes are connected to the main water supply. Some water authorities will check your plumbing and measure the amount of lead present. If levels are high, consider replacing pipes. Using a **water filter** is an effective means of reducing lead; change filters regularly. As a precaution, run the tap for a few minutes in the morning to clear water that has been left standing in pipes overnight; use water from the cold tap for drinking and cooking. To reduce the risk of lead being absorbed by food in cans, check that the manufacturer uses tin-free steel that needs no soldering, and never buy food in dented, damaged, or rusty cans.

**Light bulbs** Electricity bills and **energy** consumption can both be reduced by using **low-energy bulbs**. These com-

90

pact, fluorescent bulbs for **incandescent** and **fluorescent lights** use 80 percent less energy than standard bulbs. Low-energy bulbs cost more initially, but their longer life - up to eight times longer than standard bulbs – means that they very quickly pay for themselves. Low-energy lighting also creates less pollution: a low-energy bulb produces around one-sixth of the **carbon dioxide ($CO_2$)** of a standard 60 watt bulb. These bulbs are particularly economic in places, such a hallways, where lights are kept on for long periods. Try also **halogen lamps** in desk lights and uplighters. The small quartz glass bulbs can last around 4000 hours, but some models tested were found to emit levels of ultraviolet radiation that exceeded international-ly-agreed limits. Always remember to switch off lights when you are not using them and periodically dust shades and light fittings for maximum light. See **Halogen lamps**.

**Lighting** Many people are exposed to only small amounts of daylight, especially in the winter months, and some workspaces depend entirely on **artificial light**. Natural light is essential for health, and people who are particular-ly sensitive to inadequate daylight, suffer such unpleasant symptoms as depression and fatigue, known collectively as the SAD (Seasonal Affective Disorder) syndrome. Symptoms can be alleviated by installing **full-spectrum lighting**. This type of lighting closely resembles daylight since, as its name implies, it includes light from the ultra-violet end of the spectrum. Low levels of exposure to ultraviolet are considered beneficial, but people who are especially vulnerable to strong sunlight, such as children or those with skin cancer, should be protected. Full-spec-trum fluorescent bulbs are widely available. "Daylight" full-spectrum bulbs are also available for lamps, and are particularly suitable for the **home office**. **Halogen lamps**, while not full-spectrum, give out a strong, bright, white light that is close to daylight in quality and are **energy efficient**. The greatest saving on lighting bills can be made by investing in compact, fluorescent, **low-energy bulbs** for both incandescent and fluorescent fittings. Low-energy bulbs use 75 percent less energy than standard bulbs, and although initially more expensive, they last up to eight times longer. They also create less **carbon dioxide ($CO_2$)**. The older type of fluorescent tube, however, has a **ballast** (starting mechanism) that is less efficient, uses more energy, and causes more flickering. Ballasts in pre-1978 **fluorescent lights** may also pollute indoor air by releasing toxic **PCBs**. Carefully replace old fixtures with new, compact fluorescents. Always turn off lights when you are not using them, and keep bulbs and lamp-shades clean.

**Lignin paste** Nontoxic lignin is a natural adhesive made from the deposits in woody plant stems, and is suitable for **linoleum** and **cork** products. Lignin paste contains no **solvents** so does not give off harmful vapors.

**Lime** This **softwood** grows in the UK and Europe and is a **sustainable timber**. See the list on p. 155.

**Lignin paste**
**Lime**
**Limewash**
**Limonene**
**Lindane**

**Limewash** This paste, made from slaked lime (calcium hydroxide) and **water**, is also known as **whitewash**. A natural antiseptic that deters insects, limewash is used extensively in Mediterranean countries as an exterior and interior **paint**, and is appropriate for areas where food is kept. It is easy to apply and is suitable for dry spaces where there is a large area of wall or ceiling to cover. Limewash, however, flakes easily, and, being neither durable nor washable, will need to be reapplied more frequently than synthetic paints. Limewash is inexpensive, nontoxic, dries quickly, and has a pleasant smell.

**Limonene** A synthetic fragrance that gives a "lemon" scent to such products as **air freshener**, limonene is a suspected carcinogen. See **Air freshener** for safer alternatives, and use **essential oil** of lemon, or pure lemon juice instead.

**Lindane** Lindane is the common name of the **insecticide Gamma HCH** or Gamma BHC, a **chlorinated hydrocarbon** that kills woodworm and is widely used in garden insecticides and in **timber treatments** for rot. Lindane is highly poisonous if swallowed, and can be absorbed through the skin. Lindane causes cancer of the liver in laboratory animals and is a suspected human carcinogen. There has been a high incidence of leukemia among timber treatment workers exposed to this chemical. In homes and schools sprayed with lindane-based treatments, a variety of unpleasant symptoms have been reported. These range from severe headaches, nausea, and poor concentration, to more serious long-term effects including liver and kidney damage, aplastic anemia, and epilepsy. In the body, lindane accumulates in fat stores where it can remain for a long time after initial exposure. Lindane was banned in Sweden in 1969; in the US, the Environmental Protection Agency has classed it as a carcinogen and strictly limited its use; and it is also banned or severely restricted in Bulgaria, Colombia, Finland, Hungary, Japan, Portugal, and Thailand. Avoid products containing it and see **Timber treatments** and **Wood preservative** for alternatives.

**Linoleum** This is a mixture of powdered **cork**, **linseed oil**, wood resin, wood flour, and chalk, which, backed with **hessian**, makes a good, natural **flooring** material. Linoleum is strong and flexible but must be laid only where floor surfaces are free from moisture, so that the hessian backing does not become moist and disintegrate. Use such nontoxic **adhesives** as **lignin paste** with linoleum.

**Linseed oil** A pale yellow oil with a distinctive odor, linseed oil is pressed from flax seed. It was formerly the main ingredient of **varnishes**, and was mixed with pigments and natural **turpentine** to make decorators' oil **paint**. It is also an ingredient of **linoleum**, and, because it nourishes **wood**, is found in good quality **furniture polish**. Now, linseed oil forms the basis of **organic paint**, but in commercial brands soya oil or safflower oil are preferred alternatives since they give off less odor. See **Polish** for recipes using linseed oil.

**Liquefied petroleum gas (LPG)** This liquid gas is stored under pressure in heavy metal cylinders and is used for cooking and heating in areas where there is no main-fed natural **gas** supply. Natural gas is made of **methane**, but LPG is either **butane** or **propane**.

**Loft insulation** See **Insulation**.

**Low-energy bulbs** See **Light bulbs** and **Lighting**.

**Low-flush toilet** See **Dual-flush toilet**.

**Lye** This is one of the common names for **sodium hydroxide**, a caustic and irritant chemical found in **drain cleaner** and some **oven cleaner**. Lye is also known as **caustic soda**.

**Mahogany** Due to demand and the unsustainable management of forests, supplies of this **tropical hardwood** are rapidly becoming exhausted. Avoid products made from mahogany. Choose **sustainable timber** products and **softwood** alternatives. See the list on p. 155.

**Manganese** This metal occurs naturally in the **water** supplies of some regions and may discolor tap water. Normal levels of manganese do not make water unsafe to drink, but, if you are concerned, use a **water filter**.

**Maple** This temperate **hardwood** is grown in Europe and North America. Maple is a **sustainable timber** and is used for **furniture** and **flooring**. See the list on p. 155.

**Medicine cabinet** Always keep medicine cabinets containing drugs locked and out of the reach of children. Return any medications you no longer require to your doctor or pharmacist for safe disposal; do not flush them down the **toilet** to contaminate **water** supplies. For minor ailments, consider using herbal and homeopathic remedies. The manufacturing process of such natural remedies creates less pollution than the pharmaceutical industry.

**Medium Density Fiberboard (MDF)** In common with all **board** products, MDF contains a **urea formaldehyde** resin to bind together the wood fibers. Formaldehyde is a sus-

pected carcinogen that will **outgas** from the board, especially when new. Choose **softwoods** such as **pine** for
shelving and furniture. See also **Board**.

**Melamine formaldehyde** Melamine, a **plastic** resin, is used
to coat and protect **wood**. As a finish it is not hazardous,
but will give off highly toxic fumes at high temperatures
and when burning. Melamine is, however, also combined
with hazardous **formaldehyde** to produce melamine
formaldehyde, a compound that is used to treat **board**
products and to give **fabric** a **fire-retardant** finish.

**Meranti** This **tropical hardwood** is an endangered rainforest
**timber**, so avoid products made from meranti unless supplied from managed plantations. Choose alternatives from
the list of **sustainable timber** on p. 155.

**Merbau** This **tropical hardwood** is an endangered **timber**.
Unless they originate from managed plantations, avoid
products made from merbau. See the list of **sustainable
timber** on p. 155 for alternatives.

Melamine
formaldehyde
Meranti
Merbau
Mercury
Metal cleaner/
polish

**Mercury** This silver-colored metal is commonly used in
**thermometers** and barometers. It is highly toxic if swallowed or absorbed through the skin. Mercury is found in
**batteries** and has leached into drinking **water** supplies near
landfills where used batteries have been dumped. Mercury
accumulates in body tissues, and low levels may cause
anxiety, depression, and impaired co-ordination of the
limbs. Choose mercury-free batteries and treat older batteries as **hazardous waste**. If a thermometer or barometer
breaks, wear gloves when sweeping up the mercury, put it
in a sealed container, and take it to a pharmacy, or to your
hazardous waste disposal center.

**Metal cleaner/polish** Many metal cleaners contain **sulphuric
acid**, a toxic, corrosive substance that causes severe burns
and gives off harmful fumes. **Ammonia** is another common
ingredient that also emits irritant chemical vapors. Metal
cleaners pollute the **water** supply so never empty partially-
used containers down the drain. There are safer and
cheaper ways to clean metals that do not pollute the environment. For silver cutlery, lay a sheet of **aluminum foil** or
a dozen foil bottle tops in a pan, cover with 2-3in of water

then add 1 tsp salt and 1 tsp of **bicarbonate of soda**. Bring to the boil, drop in the cutlery, boil for 5 min, then remove and rinse. For silver jewelery, shred enough aluminum foil to half-fill a glass jar. Add 1 tbsp salt and fill with water. Drop in jewelery, cover jar, leave for 5 min, then remove and rinse. **Washing soda** will also clean silver: put foil or foil bottle tops in a pan, add water, 1 tbsp washing soda, and the silver, then simmer for 5 mins. Brass and copper can be cleaned with a paste of equal parts of lemon juice and salt; with a lemon wedge coated in bicarbonate of soda; with hot white **vinegar** and salt; or with a mixture of vinegar and bicarbonate of soda.

**Methane** This **hydrocarbon** is the principal constituent of natural **gas**. Methane is toxic only in very large amounts in confined spaces. Natural gas causes less atmospheric pollution than coal – burned in power stations to supply electricity – or oil, and is a more cost-efficient method of heating. Methane is, however, increasing in the atmosphere and is contributing to the **greenhouse effect:** as a greenhouse gas it is 20 times more potent than **carbon dioxide ($CO_2$)**. Methane is a naturally occurring gas, that is given off principally by rotting vegetation, and by ruminating animals – methane is present in their gut-bacteria and is expelled into the air. Another source of methane is organic matter from domestic **waste** that is left to decompose in landfills. Methane combines with carbon dioxide to form a dangerous mixture that can build up and cause an explosion. Methane can, however, be safely trapped and then burned as a source of **energy**.

**Methanol** A **solvent**, known also as **methyl alcohol**, methanol is used in **de-icer**, **paint stripper**, and **varnish** remover. Methanol is flammable and highly toxic. Exposure to methanol harms the optic nerve and may lead to loss of sight. Methanol slowly builds up in body tissues via inhalation or absorption through the skin, and can accumulate to harmful levels. When using products containing methanol, wear gloves, protect your eyes, and be sure that there is plenty of **ventilation**. In the US, methanol may soon be used as a fuel for buses, to reduce smog. See **Paint stripper**, **De-icer** for safer alternatives.

**Methyl alcohol** See **Methanol**.

**Methyl chloroform** See **1,1,1-Trichloroethane**.

**Methylated spirit** See **Ethanol**.

**Methylene chloride** See **Dichloromethane**.

**Microwave** Microwave ovens heat food by passing microwaves – short- to medium-wave electromagnetic radiation – through it. Microwaves are particularly suitable for frozen and cook-chill convenience foods. Such foods, however, may be contaminated with bacteria, notably listeria. These bacteria can cause food poisoning, and cooking food in microwaves may not destroy them. A recent UK government report showed that a third of the microwave ovens tested did not heat mashed potatoes through to the temperature designed to kill bacteria. Pregnant women, elderly people, and those with a low resistance to infection are particularly at risk from food poisoning and more so when raw poultry and convenience foods are improperly cooked. Stirring the food or rotating the dish during the cooking process helps to distribute microwave heat evenly. Public concern still exists, as well, over the possibility of leaks from badly-sealed microwave doors, so be sure that your oven is properly maintained. If you are in the high-risk group, the Consumers' Association advise against this method of cooking poultry and cook-chill foods. Fresh food is healthier than convenience food, but if you are short of time consider using other rapid-cooking methods such as a **pressure cooker** for boiling, or a wok for stir frying.

Methyl chloroform
Methylated spirit
Methylene chloride
Microwave
Mineral water
Mineral wool

**Mineral water** See **Bottled water**.

**Mineral wool** This **insulation material** is usually composed of glass fiber or rock wool, and is suitable for attics. Always wear a mask to protect your lungs from the sharp fibers when laying down sheets of mineral wool. These fibers can also cut your hands so wear work, not knitted, gloves. Studies of people working on the production of mineral fibers have implicated these materials in the causation of lung cancer. Some types of mineral fiber also contain **formaldehyde**, another suspected carcinogen. Consider using **vermiculite** chips as a safer alternative.

**Moisture** In the home moisture can ruin interior decoration and, at a more serious level, it can be a sign of structural problems. There are three types of moisture: penetrating moisture, rising moisture, and **condensation.** The **basement** (p. 50) in particular can be vulnerable and it is important to provide adequate **ventilation** and **insulation** in this part of the house. Leaving damp basements unchecked can mean relaying and waterproofing the whole floor area.

**Moisture**

Penetrating moisture seeps through from outside the house, usually appearing on the inside as an isolated damp patch, situated above floor level. Water penetration through the wall can be caused by defective gutters and downspouts; by leaks around the doors or **windows**; by missing shingles, roof tiles, or slates; or because brick walls need repointing. To remedy this type of moisture, replace defective downspouts and gutters, check seals, replace missing shingles, or roof tiles, or slates, and repoint brick walls. If the cause is not obvious, consider siding the outside wall with boarding, for example. If the internal area is very damp, consider using a **dehumidifier**.

Rising moisture is indicated by a tide mark on the inside walls above floor level. It occurs when the **damp proof course (DPC)** is old and inadequate, or when the DPC has been "bridged" either on the outside or on the inside. Bridging on the outside may be due to rendering or stucco extending down below the line of the DPC, or soil accumulating above it. Interior bridging may be due to plasterwork that has extended below the level of the DPC. Check that external rendering or internal plastering stop above the DPC, and that there are no other obstructions. If there is no DPC, or it is defective, have one professionally installed. There are two kinds of DPC, both consisting of a barrier: the first type is a physical barrier made from **aluminum**, **lead**, **bitumen**, **felt**, or **plastic**; in more modern homes, this is like a termite shield. The second type is a chemical barrier. See **Damp proofing fluid**.

Condensation occurs, for example, when the temperature of the outside surfaces of walls and windows is much cooler than the temperature on the inside. This causes the moisture in the air to condense and form droplets of water. Condensation is often found in such humid areas as the **kitchen** (p. 16) and **bathroom** (p. 80), especially if there is inadequate ventilation due to excessive **weather-**

**stripping**, too much insulation, and even **double glazing** with metal-framed windows. Remedies for condensation include opening windows and installing an **extractor fan**. Take the general precaution of ensuring that there is enough ventilation in the attic space and that there is minimum heating in very cold rooms. As a last resort for severe condensation, use a dehumidifier.

**Mold** This fungus is a sure indication of moisture, and its musty-smelling spores, drifting through indoor air, can trigger allergic reactions. Mold is encouraged by **condensation** in poorly-ventilated **bathrooms** (p. 80), **kitchens** (p. 16), and **basements** (p. 50). Condensation is also produced by **bottled gas** heaters. To prevent mold from spreading, check the house for leaks, seal any cracks, and thoroughly clean kitchens and bathrooms. Be sure that there is plenty of **ventilation**, remove excess moisture from the air, by opening windows and perhaps installing an **extractor fan**. A **dehumidifier** will help with a particularly damp area, or you can buy small refillable containers filled with moisture-absorbing crystals. The standing water in these appliances can, however, rapidly turn into a breeding ground for bacteria, so empty them regularly. **Borax** inhibits the growth of mold: clean kitchen walls, and bathroom fittings and floors, with a nontoxic solution of borax and **water** (1 part borax to 8 parts water). This solution will also eliminate stains once mold has formed.

Mold
Mosquito repellent
Mothballs and Mothproofer

**Mosquito repellent** See **Insect repellent**.

**Mothballs and Mothproofer** Products for deterring or killing moths commonly contain **naphthalene**, a toxic **petrochemical** that gives off irritant fumes. Others contain hazardous **para-dichlorobenzene**, a powerful respiratory irritant that can cause long-term damage to kidneys and liver. Very low concentrations of naphthalene poison aquatic life, and mothproofer **aerosol** sprays may contain **CFCs** that damage the **ozone** layer. Treat mothballs and mothproofer as **hazardous waste**; do not put them in the **trashbin**. **Herbs** that repel moths make safer, nontoxic alternatives, and they do not harm the environment. Hang sachets of cedar chips, dried lavender, southernwood, or rosemary in cupboards. Get rid of any moth eggs on clothes by pressing with a hot steam iron, or by tumble drying.

99

**Naphtha** Naphtha is a narcotic substance that causes drowsiness and stupor when inhaled. Used in such products as paint brush restorer, naphtha is also flammable. When using products containing this **solvent**, always replace caps.

**Naphthalene** This aromatic **hydrocarbon**, derived from **petroleum**, is the common active ingredient of **mothballs and mothproofer**. Naphthalene is toxic if repeatedly inhaled or absorbed through the skin, and is a suspected animal carcinogen. It is also poisonous to fish and other aquatic life, so see **hazardous waste** for disposal.

**Neutralizing undersheet** This reinforced, **aluminum** sheet is normally fitted under the **mattress** to shield you from **electromagnetic fields (EMFs)** while you sleep. EMFs are given off by household wiring, electrical appliances, and also via metal springs in a **mattress** if they become magnetized; they are considered injurious to health by some authorities. It is claimed that the neutralizing undersheet will shield you from between 90 and 95 percent of EMFs and result in a healthier and more refreshing night's sleep. The sheet is normally placed under your mattress and is fitted with an grounding wire that diverts EMFs from the body to the undersheet where they are neutralized. The sheet is connected to a socket with a standard plug, or may be attached to a bare water or **gas** pipe.

**Nicotine** This is one of several toxic compounds present in **tobacco smoke**. It causes cancer and birth defects in animals, and is rapidly absorbed through the skin. Nicotine is also used as a garden **insecticide**. If you smoke in your home, use one well-ventilated room only and consider investing in an **air cleaner** or an **ionizer** to reduce levels of pollutants; a group of **house plants** should also help.

**Nitrates** These nitrogen fertilizers are used by gardeners and farmers to maintain high crop yields. In intensive agricultural areas, nitrates can leach into rivers and groundwater supplies and contaminate tap water. At high levels, nitrates increase the risk of a rare blood disease, known as "blue baby syndrome", that can affect babies whose bottle formulas are made up with tap water. In the body, nitrates break down and undergo chemical changes into substances that have caused cancer in animals. Studies have also suggested a link between nitrates and stomach and oesophagal cancers in humans. Treatments to remove nitrates from water supplies on a large scale are still being developed. If, however, you live in an area of intensive arable farming, invest in a **water filter**. You will normally have to buy a separate nitrate-reducing unit, although at least one type of jug-filter that claims to reduce nitrate levels. Another, more expensive, option is to use **bottled water** for drinking and babies' formula. Although not nitrate-free, tests have shown that bottled water is likely to have less than half the nitrate levels of tap water from intensively agricultural regions. Food – grains, fruit, and vegetables – that has been grown with nitrogen fertilizers may also contain high levels of nitrates. Choose instead **organic** food that is grown without the use of chemical fertilizers. Compost and manure are good, safe alternatives to nitrate fertilizers for your garden.

**Nitric oxide** See **Nitrogen oxides**.

**Nitrocellulose** All **cellulose** paints contain nitrocellulose, an ingredient which is thought to have a stimulant effect on the heart. Do not breathe the vapor from this type of paint, especially if you suffer from heart problems. Such paint is used in DIY modelling work and also as a spray paint for cars. Cellulose paint commonly contains **solvents** and these may also emit harmful vapors. Nitrocellulose is also highly flammable, especially when dry, so always replace the lid on paint cans, do not let the paint dry out, and keep away from sources of ignition. Avoid models or toys that require paints containing nitrocellulose.

**Nitrogen dioxide** See **Nitrogen oxides**.

**Nitrogen oxides (NOx)** This collective term describes two pollutant **combustion gases**, **nitric oxide (NO)** and **nitrogen dioxide (NO$_2$)**. These gases are given off when fossil fuels (**coal**, oil, and **gas**) are burnt in power stations, in vehicle internal combustion engines, and in gas **stoves** and heaters. They are also present in **tobacco smoke**. NO is a colorless, odorless, tasteless gas that converts to NO$_2$ when mixed with oxygen. NO$_2$ is a toxic, irritant gas that aggravates the respiratory system and can destroy lung tissue. Emissions of NO$_2$ also damage the environment by combining with water vapor to form **acid rain**. To reduce levels of nitrogen oxides in the home, check that gas stoves and heaters are burning efficiently, and have them regularly serviced. If you smoke, set aside a room for this purpose and make sure that there is plenty of **ventilation**. **House plants**, especially spider plants, *Chlorophytum elatum* var. *vittatum*, are also efficient absorbers of pollutants from tobacco smoke. Atmospheric pollution from vehicle exhausts can be cut dramatically by fitting a three-way **catalytic converter** to your car. Catalytic converters reduce emissions of nitrogen oxides and other pollutant gases by as much as 90 percent. You can also help to reduce levels of nitrogen oxide pollution from power stations by cutting your electricity consumption: adopt **energy-saving** measures and use **energy-efficient** appliances.

**"Non-iron"** Fabrics and clothing with this label have been treated with a **formaldehyde** finish that binds to the fabric and is virtually impossible to wash out. Formaldehyde is a suspected carcinogen. Avoid non-iron fabrics, especially for bed linen, if you are sensitive to chemical vapor. Choose such natural alternatives as **cotton** flannel, which does not crease.

**Non-stick** Pans and other **cookware** can be coated with a **plastic** to make them non-stick. These plastic coatings gradually wear off, and particles are deposited in food.

**Nitrogen dioxide**
**Nitrogen oxides (NOx)**
**"Non-iron"**
**Non-stick**

Some are known to give off unpleasant fumes when on a high flame. Cast-iron pans are a healthier, non-stick choice, but first season them by heating half a cup of **vinegar** and 1 tbsp salt over a low flame for 30 mins. Clean the pans with absorbent kitchen **paper** towels, and oil lightly before putting away. If they get very dirty, rub with salt; do not use scouring pads.

**NTA** Nitrilotriacetic acid was formerly used in **laundry powders** as a substitute for **phosphates**. It is still used in Holland and Switzerland but was banned in the UK because it takes up toxic heavy metals already in **water** supplies, and reintroduces them into the environment. These compounds find their way into drinking water supplies and enter the food chain after being taken up by fish. Another substance, **EDTA**, has been substituted for NTA, but this poses similar environmental problems. See **Laundry powders** for fully **biodegradable** alternatives.

**Oak** This is a temperate **hardwood** that is grown in Europe, North America, and Japan. Oak is strong and durable, and is a **sustainable timber** much used in construction, furniture-making, and joinery. See the list of sustainable timbers on p. 155.

**Okoume** This endangered **tropical hardwood** is also known as **gaboon**. Avoid products made from okoume unless **timber** supplies come from **sustainable** sources. See the list of **sustainable timber** on p. 155 for alternatives.

**Optical brighteners** As the name suggests, optical brighteners or whiteners, are used in **laundry powder** to make your laundry appear whiter. They may also be found in **toothpaste** and some **paper** products, and were formerly used in white sugar and flour until banned. Once the brighteners have bound themselves to **fabrics** during washing, they achieve a whitening effect by converting the invisible ultraviolet light in daylight to visible bluish light. The optical illusion created by the fluorescent, blue-reflected light makes whites appear whiter, although, in fact, your laundry is not any cleaner. Optical brighteners are said to be responsible for skin allergies, and they are not fully **biodegradable**. See **Laundry powder** for alternative products without brighteners.

**Organic** This term, when applied to food, describes the methods used in the growing process. Organic produce is grown without using chemical fertilizers, synthetic **pesticides**, and herbicides. In organic culture, priority is given to the long-term health of the soil. Weeds and pests are kept down by using such methods as crop rotation and companion planting or intercropping (planting different types of plants together), and the plants are thus better equipped to resist disease than would be the case if they were sprayed. The term organic is also used to describe meat from animals that have been reared without antibiotics or growth hormones. Organic growers may employ pesticides but they would be plant- or animal- not chemical-based. Fertilizers added to the soil would also be of plant or animal origin, manure, for example, not synthetic **nitrates**. Organic produce is not, of course, invulnerable to the effects of national and global atmospheric pollution, but is comparatively free from chemical residues. Organic produce is generally less processed than non-organic food and contributes to the health of the land and to the conservation of the countryside.

**Organic**
**Organic chemicals**
**Organic paint**
**Organochlorines**

**Organic chemicals** This generic term is applied to chemicals based on carbon, but does not include the simpler compounds such as **carbon dioxide** and **carbon monoxide**. Inorganic chemicals are those based on elements other than carbon, and would include compounds of, for example, **cadmium** and **mercury**.

**Organic paint** See **Paint, organic**.

**Organochlorines** The term **chlorinated hydrocarbons** is interchangeable with organochlorines – a group of **organic** chemicals that contain carbon linked directly with **chlorine**. Common substances in the organochlorine group include such **solvents** as **dichloromethane** and **trichloroethylene**, plus **lindane**, a hazardous **insecticide**. Generally speaking, organochlorines are toxic substances and lindane is one of the most dangerous of the group. Organochlorines are stored in body fat and, because they are not **biodegradable**, they also persist in the environment. When heated or burned, fumes from organochlorine solvents form a toxic gas. See also **Solvents**.

**Outgas** This term means to give off potentially harmful gas or vapor, and is in common use in the US. The outgassing process is stimulated by heat and light. Products that outgas include **board**, such as **chipboard** and **plywood** and certain types of **plastic** and synthetics, such as **PVC**. The resulting vapor can contaminate indoor air, cause discomfort to the chemically sensitive, and some are suspected carcinogens, for example **formaldehyde**.

**Oven cleaner** The common active ingredient of many oven cleaners is **sodium hydroxide (caustic soda)**. Caustic soda is a corrosive substance that irritates the eyes, the skin, and the mucous membranes, even when much diluted. It is also harmful to fish and plant life, so do not dispose of oven cleaner down the drain. **Aerosol** oven cleaners based on caustic soda are particularly hazardous since, in this form, the chemical vapor is more likely to get into your eyes. Never use oven cleaners at the same time as cleaning products containing **ammonia**: poisonous ammonia gas will be released. A safer alternative is to wet the oven walls and base thoroughly after use to soften baked-on food and grease. Scrub off with wire wool and clean with a solution of 1 tbsp **bicarbonate of soda** to a half-pint of water. Another method you can use is to sprinkle salt on spills, leave the area to cool, and then scrub off. A nontoxic commercial cleaner is also available for ceramic, glass, and halogen burner eyes.

**Oxalic acid** This acid may be an ingredient of products that are used to restore the color of wood. Avoid inhaling such products, wear gloves, and keep them off your skin and away from your eyes.

**Oxygen bleach** There are two types of bleach, those based on **chlorine**, and the oxygen variety, usually based on **hydrogen peroxide** or **sodium percarbonate**. Oxygen bleaches break down more rapidly than chlorine bleaches, and are less harmful to the water supply and to septic tanks. Use oxygen bleach sparingly as, like any bleach, it can irritate your eyes and skin and is harmful if swallowed. For alternatives to bleach for **toilets** and sinks, try **borax** or white **vinegar**. See also **Bleach**.

**Ozone** This pungent gas is present in large quantities in the upper reaches of the atmosphere, in an area known as the ozone layer. This protective layer circles the earth and screens out harmful ultraviolet (UV) radiation that is given off by the sun, in particular most UV-B radiation. High concentrations of UV radiation cause skin cancers, cataracts, damage to crops and interfere with marine life. This fragile layer is thinning, and scientists now agree that **CFCs, halons,** and certain **solvents** are responsible. A single **aerosol** containing CFC propellants can destroy up to 3.3 tons of ozone and certain halons are even more damaging. In 1985 an ozone hole was discovered over the Antarctic, 1989 saw a marked depletion of ozone over the Arctic, and it is estimated that over such densely-populated parts of the northern hemisphere as the UK, the layer has already thinned by up to eight percent. Official US statistics predict that there will be 150 million extra cases of skin cancer in white US citizens born before 2075, and that for every one percent drop in ozone levels there will be a corresponding increase of two percent in skin cancers. In 1989 the European Economic Community (EEC) agreed to ban the use of all CFCs by the end of this century and most aerosols are now CFC-free. CFCs are, however, widely used in **refrigerators,** blown-foam **packaging** made from **polystyrene**, extruded polystyrene **insulation**, computers, and **air-conditioning** systems. **1,1,1-Trichloroethane**, one of the most widely used solvents, also destroys ozone. See **CFCs** for further information.

Ozone

Ozone is also found nearer the ground where it settles in the form of a photochemical smog. Car exhausts emit **nitrogen oxides** and such **hydrocarbons** as **benzene**. These substances then react with sunlight to produce an ozone smog that can increase the risk of lung cancer. Some electrical equipment such as **photocopiers** and **computers** also give out ozone. In a badly-ventilated room where a photocopier is running, ozone concentrations can build up to potentially harmful levels. To reduce the incidence of ozone at ground level, use the car less and make sure it's equipped with a **catalytic converter**; and see that photocopiers are sited in well-ventilated spaces.

**Packaging** Packaging protects goods, displays information, and helps market the product. Most, however, is thrown away, never to be reused. In the US, packaging materials account for 65 percent of what is thrown away each day. With the advent of **plastic**, and self-service stores, the volume of packaging materials increased dramatically, bringing in its wake large quantities of litter. While packaging costs are included in the purchase price of a product, there is an additional, hidden, cost of disposal. Packaging is expensive: the extraction and processing of raw materials for **aluminum** and **glass** use vast amounts of **energy** and may cause environmental damage; the costs of transporting such materials are high; and finally the finding of sites to dump large quantities of waste packaging is becoming increasingly difficult and costly. Some kinds of blown **polyurethane foam** packaging, commonly used for fast food, eggs, and hot drinks, also contain **ozone**-damaging **CFCs**. In most European countries other than the UK, cutting down on packaging and waste is a top priority. In Italy over 200 communities have banned the use of plastic bags; in Sweden there is a tax on non-returnable drinks containers and a program for returnable ones; French supermarkets sell beer in standard refillable **bottles** that can be taken back for cleaning and filling.

The key to cutting down on packaging is, first, to buy products wrapped in materials suitable for **recycling**, or that have refillable and reusable containers; and, second, to avoid overpackaged goods. Choosing products in these ways may persuade product designers to use less packaging, and to use a greater proportion of materials that can be recycled. Ideally, the composition of the packaging material of a product, for example drink **cans**, would be clearly identified to facilitate separation of different materials before recycling. Products made of a single metal or type of plastic would make recycling even easier. Beware of packaging that is deceptive of the size or quantity of the contents.

**Padauk**
**Paint**

### Steps you can take to reduce packaging

- Avoid such overpackaged items as supermarket vegetables on a plastic tray covered in **clingfilm**. Remember that you are paying for the packaging and that it is usually cheaper to buy vegetables loose.
- When shopping, take your own shopping bag and don't accept plastic bags. If you need a carrier bag, ask for a paper one.
- Buy goods wrapped in materials that can be recycled, and recycle everything you can. Glass, for instance, can be recycled over and over again. See also **Recycling**.
- Buy products that come in reusable and refillable containers. Have your milk delivered or, if there is no delivery service, buy it in bottles, not cartons. The average UK milk bottle is reused 24 times.

**Padauk** This **tropical hardwood** is an endangered **timber**. Avoid products made from padauk unless supplies come from managed plantations. See the list of **sustainable timber** on p. 155 for alternatives.

**Paint** The two basic types of paint used in home decorating are water-based, or **emulsion paint**, and oil-based (alkyd), or **gloss paint**. Both types are manufactured using non-renewable **petrochemicals**. Paint contains a variety of ingredients including white **pigment** – formerly **lead** but now usually **titanium dioxide** – plus colored pigments. Lead was also used as a drying agent in paint, and although most paint in the US is now labeled "contains no lead", certain specialty paints may still contain a small proportion. Toxic **cadmium** is often used as an alternative drying agent. Resinous synthetic binders are added to keep the pigment smoothly dispersed and give the paint a film. These are called alkyds and are formed by the reaction of an oil, usually soya oil, with chemical additives to form polymers or chains. **Solvents** are also used to keep the paint flowing smoothly, although emulsion paint contains much smaller amounts of solvent than gloss. For flexibility and durability, and to make paint washable, certain types of **plastic** are added to paint including **vinyl**, **acrylic**, and **PVC**. Other chemical additives include **fungicides** that are designed to remain active once the paint has dried, plus preservatives. The constituents of paint are, therefore, complex, and oil-based paints, in particular, have a high content of potentially toxic and/or allergenic substances. Paint manufacturers themselves give clear indications of the potentially harmful solvent vapors by advising you to apply paint in areas that are well ventilated. In fact, a UK study of professional painters working with solvent-based paints found that 93 percent showed symptoms of solvent poisoning. Many people are also sensitive to the chemical and plastic vapors given off by paint, both on application and as it dries, and these substances can continue to **outgas** even when the paint is dry. Symptoms include drowsiness, headaches, and respiratory problems. Low-odor paints are preferable, especially for the **nursery** (p.144), but these are not entirely solvent free. In 1987, some US paint manufacturers began developing reduced volatile organic compound (VOC) paints to comply with EPA regulations on specialty coatings. Currently, Air Quality Management Districts across the country are working to determine standards on a state-by-state basis. Synthetic paint with plastic additives also seals surfaces to such an extent that walls, ceilings, and **wood** cannot "breathe". This prevents the evaporation of any moisture.

If you would prefer not to be exposed to the chemicals and plastics in paint, choose water-based emulsions, **casein** emulsion, and simple **limewash** or **distemper**. You can also make your own paint by mixing casein emulsion, limewash, or distemper with artists' pigments. See **Paint, organic** for safe alternatives.

**Paint, exterior** Masonry paint is usually offered in three textures smooth, textured, and thick bodied. The thicker texture is achieved by adding fine particles of sand, stone, or **granite**. This type of paint contains **mold** inhibitors, usually **dodecyclamine**, an irritant. Exterior undercoat and

**Paint, exterior**

gloss paints for **wood** also commonly contain **solvents**, **fungicides**, and mold inhibitors. Manufacturers advise against inhaling the vapors, getting splashes on your skin, and pouring unused paint down drains or into water-courses. See **Paint, organic** for alternatives.

**Paint, organic** Organic paint is made from purely natural materials including plant oils, particularly **linseed oil**, resins, and minerals. It does not contain synthetic **petro-chemical** additives, **plastic**, or **solvents**. The absence of plastics means that surfaces covered with organic paint allow air to pass through them, and moisture to evaporate. This enables your home to "breathe" and improves the indoor climate. Since no solvents or chemical additives **outgas** from this type of paint at any stage, your home is not contaminated with unpleasant and potentially harmful fumes. It is therefore ideal for people with chemical sensitivities or for rooms where babies and young children sleep and play. Organic paint is available in **emulsion** and oil-based varieties. A basic, white emulsion is offered, to which you add your own choice of natural toning pigment to create the color you want. Or, for a special effect, cover white emulsion with a translucent plant paint. There is also a **casein** wallpaint, a chalk-based paint similar to **limewash**, and an emulsion binder that you add to emulsion paint for extra durability. Organic, oil-based paint for **wood**, stone and metal surfaces comes in various colors created by adding earth **pigments**. Exterior **gloss paint**, and an organic masonry paint for exterior stone and plaster, are available, although the masonry paint requires skilled application. For priming surfaces, including metal, there is a nontoxic **primer**.

**Paint stripper** Probably one of the most toxic home-decorating products, paint stripper contains such dangerous **solvents** as **dichloromethane (methylene chloride)** and often **sodium hydroxide**. Dichloromethane gives off toxic fumes, and will burn the skin. If the fumes are inhaled near sources of ignition, poisonous **phosgene** gas is emitted. Avoid such toxic paint strippers and choose instead safer products, that contain no dichloromethane, or caustic soda, and contain reduced volatile organic compounds (VOCs) or are fume-free. Organic paint suppliers also offer a safer paint-stripping paste.

**Paint, organic**
**Paint stripper**

**Paint thinner** Before the advent of synthetics, pure **turpentine**, distilled from **pine** resin, was used to thin paint. Now this has been replaced by products derived from **petrochemicals**, including turpentine substitute and **white spirit**. These products are highly flammable and irritant. Prolonged exposure to white spirit is associated with dermatitis and severe damage to the nervous system. If you are using such paint thinners, ensure that windows are open, do not inhale the fumes, and keep the products off your skin. Pure turpentine is safer, as is a thinner derived from citrus oils offered by organic paint suppliers. This natural thinner is free from **pesticides**, has a shorter drying time than white spirit, turpentine substitute, or pure turpentine, and can be used to clean brushes. It is recommended for those who are sensitive to turpentine.

**Paper** It has been estimated that some 90 million trees are cut down each year to satisfy just the UK demand for paper and board. In the US, junk mail alone is responsible for the felling of 10 million trees each year. Each person in the UK uses two trees' worth of paper and board per annum and the average UK household throws away around 6.5 pounds of paper per week. Trees absorb **carbon dioxide ($CO_2$)** when growing and therefore help to slow down the **greenhouse effect**, so cutting trees for paper effectively leads to the increase of $CO_2$ in the atmosphere. Extensive conifer plantations in unsuitable environments cause ecological problems too, including increased soil acidity. Paper can easily be recycled: 50 percent of the paper used in Japan and Holland is recycled, but in the UK the figure is only 29 percent. In several US states, newspapers must, by law, contain at least 40 percent of recycled paper. In 1987 in the UK, just 386,000 tons of newspapers were recycled, while 1.8 million tons were thrown away. **Recycling** waste paper to make new paper is clearly economic: it represents an **energy saving** of between 30 and 40 percent on paper made from virgin pulp, and produces less than a quarter of the environmental pollution. The **chlorine bleach** used to whiten pulp is particularly polluting since the process produces toxic **dioxins** that can be discharged into rivers. Concern has been expressed about the health risks from possible dioxin-contamination of such paper products as milk cartons, coffee-filters, **sanitary protection products**, and disposable

The bedroom is where we go in search of peace and quiet, to rest, recuperate from illness, and of course to sleep – an activity that takes up a third of our lives. Since good sleep is fundamental to our health it is essential that the bedroom provides us with a healthy, restful environment. Ironically, the furniture, materials, fittings, and appliances found in most bedrooms, may themselves be the cause of disturbed sleeping patterns, irritability, and allergies.

1 Organic paint
2 Solid wood bedframe
3 Hot water bottle
4 Solid wood fittings
5 Pure cotton sheets
6 Cruelty-free cosmetics
7 Pure fleece underblanket
8 Natural wool or fiber-filled mattress
9 Herb sachet
10 Wool or cotton rug
11 Wood floor-boards
12 Window for ventilation and light
13 House plants

**Bed** Choose a bed made from a solid **softwood**, such as **pine**, and not from an endangered **hardwood**. Avoid beds with metal frames and metal springs as they can become magnetized and may interfere with the body's own **electromagnetic fields (EMFs)**, causing such symptoms as restlessness and insomnia. Opt for solid wood frames or invest in a **neutralizing undersheet** that is claimed to shield you from EMFs. You can also install a **demand switch** which cuts off the electric current at night.

**Mattress and pillows** A sprung mattress with metal springs may set up EMFs and increase electromagnetic radiation levels. Avoid mattresses and pillows filled with **polyurethane foam**: if they catch fire, the foam gives off suffocating, toxic fumes. Healthier alternatives are a natural **wool** or fiber-filled mattress or **futon**, or a mattress made from non-allergenic **latex**.

**Bedding** All bedding made from **poly-cotton** will have been treated with **formaldehyde**, a suspected carcinogen which is used to prevent fabric creasing. Always wash new bed linen thoroughly before use. Untreated **cotton** and cotton flannel are good choices for sheets. Cotton is more absorbent than synthetic fabrics and cotton flannel is usually untreated.

**Electric blanket** Studies have found that miscarriages occur more frequently with women who use electric blankets. The electrical current may interfere with the body's electromagnetic field. Use a hot water bottle or a pure fleece underblanket instead.

112

**Bedroom furniture** Often bedroom furniture is made from **composite boards**. These boards may present health risks, due to the formaldehyde resin used in their production. Formaldehyde can **outgas**, emitting harmful fumes into the room. "Low-emission" boards may soon be available for shelving, and these should be used with nontoxic adhesives. Choose instead solid **wood** bedroom furniture made from a fast-growing softwood, such as pine, or a temperate hardwood such as **beech** or **ash**. Always avoid using endangered **tropical hardwoods**.

**Paint** Paint is usually made with polluting, synthetic **petrochemicals**. It contains volatile, harmful **solvents** and **fungicides** that can emit harmful vapors during application, while drying, and even long afterward. Synthetic paint is also a fire risk. Try natural **organic paint** or water-based **emulsion**, although the latter is a synthetic product and will contain a fungicide. Check also that the paint you use is **lead** free. For children's rooms, a low odor variety is available.

**Mothballs** These powerful **insecticides** may contain toxic chemicals which can seriously damage the liver and kidneys. These chemicals emit harmful vapor that is easily inhaled. Try such natural moth-repellent **herbs** as lavender, and southernwood.

**Bedroom**

**diapers**. In response to these fears manufacturers have begun to offer unbleached products, or to change from chlorine to **oxygen bleach**. In Sweden 95 per cent of paper products are now unbleached. Environmentalists argue that high-grade, recycled paper has, however, also been subject to chemical de-inking and bleaching processes.

### Steps you can take to reduce paper consumption

- Try to use less paper and not to waste paper: use both sides of each sheet and consider reusing envelopes.
- Recycle newspapers and used paper. Writing paper, photocopying paper and computer paper are particularly valuable so remember to save **home office** supplies.
- To stop junk mail being delivered to your door, write to the Mail Preference Service to have your name taken off their lists.
- Buy recycled paper products. These include good-quality personal and office stationery, toilet tissue, facial tissues, and kitchen towels. Consider using low-grade recycled paper products whenever possible.
- If you use napkins, try cloth instead of paper. Cloth napkins can be washed and reused.

**Para-dichloro-benzene (PDCB)**
**PCBs**

**Para-dichlorobenzene (PDCB)** This **insecticide** is an ingredient in **toilet freshener blocks**. Liver injury has followed prolonged exposure to PDCB, and it is a serious **water** pollutant. PDCB has been banned in many European countries because of its toxicity. Avoid toilet blocks containing this chemical and choose from the wide range of PDCB-free varieties available. Toilet blocks are not essential, and many contain the same type of synthetic fragrances found in **air freshener**. To clean and disinfect your toilet, try white **vinegar** plus a few drops of **essential oil** of pine for a pleasant scent. A **biodegradable** cleaner is also available. See also **Toilet cleaner**.

**PCBs** There are some 209 PCBs, or **polychlorinated biphenyls**. These are highly toxic, industrial chemicals used in some types of **plastic**, electrical capacitors, transformers, and **refrigerators**. The manufacture of PCBs has now ceased, due to their persistence in the environment. Up to a third of all PCBs manufactured have found their way into the ocean and have caused widespread contamination. PCBs that were dumped in the North Sea still continue to poison dolphins, porpoises, and seals. In 1966 scientists discovered that PCBs had entered the food chain: humans can accumulate them by eating contaminated fish. PCBs are suspected carcinogens and direct exposure causes serious skin disease and liver damage. They are also associated with birth defects, hypertension, and strokes. The PCBs already manufactured have still to be disposed of. The principal method used is incineration, but this has to take place at extremely high temperatures or poisonous **dioxins** are given off. Many PCBs are, however, illegally dumped on land. In the home, PCBs were used in starting ballasts for **fluorescent lights** manufactured before 1978. If you have such an older fluorescent fixture, have it replaced or replace it yourself, but take great care and wear gloves. Take the fixture to your nearest **hazardous waste** disposal site or contact your local health authority.

**Pear** The pear is a temperate **hardwood**, native to Europe, used for carving, turning, and veneers. Pear is a **sustainable timber**. See the list of other sustainable timbers on p. 155.

**Pentachlorophenol (PCP)** Discovered in 1841, PCP is a toxic **wood preservative** also used in **timber treatments** as a **fungicide**. It is formed, as its name suggests, by reacting **chlorine** with **phenol** and contains dangerous **dioxins**. PCP is banned in many countries and has been restricted in the US since 1986 to professional use only. Blamed for around 1000 deaths worldwide, PCP is a nerve poison that causes severe skin disease (chloracne), respiratory problems, and damage to the liver, kidney, and heart. In the US it is a suspected carcinogen. PCP is particularly hazardous if absorbed through the skin, and wood objects that have been treated with PCP remain toxic for years. Some man ufacturers of wood preservatives for DIY use have replaced PCP with **acypetacs zinc**, but for safer alternatives see **Wood preservative** and **Timber treatments**.

**Perchloroethylene** A **solvent** used in **dry cleaning**, perchloroethylene, or perklone (tetrachloroethylene), gives off harmful fumes that, in high concentrations, have a narcotic effect and are irritating to the eyes and the throat. Prolonged contact with this chemical can cause dermatitis and damage vital organs. Such contact has also been linked to the development of cancer. Perchloroethylene is also an environmental pollutant: the effluent, discharged into rivers and seas, even in very low concentrations, kills aquatic life. If certain clothes have to be professionally dry cleaned, remove the plastic cover afterwards and hang them outside, or thoroughly air them by an open window, before storing in closets and wardrobes. See **Dry cleaning**.

**"Permanent press"** All **fabrics** labeled permanent press, usually **cotton** or **poly-cotton**, have been treated with **formaldehyde**, a suspected carcinogen that will not wash out. Avoid bed linen with this label if you are chemically sensitive, and choose natural, untreated fabrics such as cotton flannel. See also **"Easy care"**, **"Non-iron"**.

**"Permanent press"**
**Permethrin**
**Personal computer**

**Permethrin** Used as a **wood preservative** and garden **insecticide**, permethrin is a synthetic chemical belonging to a group called **pyrethroids**. Permethrin is less toxic to mammals than such **organochlorine** treatments as lindane and is considered acceptable by conservationists for treating lumber in lofts where bats roost. In humans, however, permethrin is associated with nervous system damage and irritations to the eyes and skin. It is considered a suspected carcinogen by the US Food and Drug Administration. Use products containing permethrin with caution, wear protective clothing, and make sure the area to be treated is well ventilated. See **Wood preservative** and **Timber treatments** for safer alternatives.

**Personal computer** Various problems are associated with working at computer screens, or **VDTs** – visual display terminals. In US studies of pregnant women working at VDTs, a higher incidence of miscarriage was established when compared with that of those working at non-video-related jobs. This may be due to the low-level radiation emitted by VDTs and the low-frequency **electromagnetic fields (EMFs)** surrounding them. These fields are strongest at the back and sides. A limited British study in 1990, however, did not find a higher incidence of miscarriage, but found a correlation between VDT use and high levels of stress. Stress-related symptoms experienced by operators included anxiety, headaches, and depression. Eye strain is another potential hazard of working in front of video screens, while repetitive strain injury (RSI) is becoming a serious problem among VDT operators. If you use a personal computer at home, minimize the risk of health hazards by taking frequent breaks, ideally for 15 minutes every hour, or a 30 minute break every two hours, and get away from the screen. Ensure that you have a good quality chair that supports the lower back, and that the keyboard is positioned at a comfortable height. Sit at least 20in back from the screen – this is easier if you have a model with a detachable keyboard. Although low-radiation computers with internal shielding have been developed in Sweden, they are not yet widely available. You can, however, reduce glare and help to prevent eyestrain by fitting a special mesh screen. Screens are also available with grounding devices to reduce radiation from EMFs, and static.

**Pesticides**
**Petrochemicals**
**Petroleum**

**Pesticides** Synthetic pesticides are chemicals designed to kill the pests and diseases that attack animals, plants, and crops. Many farmers use them regularly and some are highly toxic. Pressure from environmental groups has led to the banning of some of the most toxic, including DDT, aldrin and dieldrin, but residues of these persistent chemicals will continue to pollute rivers for many years. In the home, pesticide residues may be found in fruit and vegetables where crops have been sprayed with synthetic chemicals. Pesticides can leach into groundwater, as well as rivers, and make their way into **drinking water** supplies. Pesticides also enter the food chain and accumulate in fish and birds.

Avoid pesticides by buying **organic** produce that has not been sprayed with synthetic chemicals or artificial fertilizers. Babies and young children are particularly at risk from water and food polluted with pesticide and fertilizer residues. If you live in an area of intensive agriculture, invest in a suitable **water filter** to reduce pollutant levels in your drinking water. Check first that the filter does reduce pesticide residues; not all of them do.

**Petrochemicals** These are **organic** chemicals obtained from **petroleum** or natural **gas**.

**Petroleum** Consisting of crude oil, or mineral oil, petroleum is a naturally occurring mixture of **hydrocarbons** and other **organic** chemicals. It is thought to have been formed by decaying animal and vegetable matter, held under pressure beneath the earth's surface. Petroleum is drilled out of the ground and then distilled into a variety of gases, such as **liquefied petroleum gas** and such liquids as **gasoline** and **kerosene**.

**Phenols** A group of **aromatic compounds**, phenols are widely used in **disinfectants** and in **wood preservative**. Phenols are also employed in synthetic resins for use in hard **plastic**, **paint**, and **varnish**. Pure phenol, also known as carbolic acid, is a powerful irritant, and all phenols are corrosive and damaging to the skin and eyes. Prolonged exposure to phenols can lead to liver and kidney damage. When heated, phenols give off toxic fumes, and, when discharged into waterways, poison fish and other aquatic life. Avoid products containing phenols and phenolic compounds whenever possible. See individual product entries for safer alternatives.

**Phosgene** This toxic gas can be formed by burning or heating compounds containing **chlorine**. Used as a poison gas in the World War I, phosgene can cause serious lung damage and even death after short exposures. It is irritating to the eyes and mucous membranes. When using such chlorinated **solvents** as **dichloromethane** in **paint stripper**, do not smoke. Drawing fumes from this type of solvent through a cigarette produces phosgene gas that goes directly to the lungs.

**Phosphates** The most controversial ingredient of **laundry powder**, phosphates are used as "builders" by manufacturers to make the water softer and more alkaline, to prevent the formation of scum, and generally improve the cleaning power of **detergent**. By weight, phosphates account for about 20 to 25 percent of the total content of most laundry powders; in powders for the **dishwasher** the proportion is even higher. Once in the waterways via the drain, phosphates become serious **water** pollutants. They over-fertilize algae – tiny green microorganisms – in slow-moving rivers and lakes, causing them to multiply so rapidly that they clog the surface of the water. This prevents oxygen from reaching fish and other aquatic life. Stretches of water then become stagnant and lifeless: a process known as "eutrophication". In Europe, eutrophication problems in

Swiss lakes led to the complete banning of phosphates in detergents. They are severely restricted in Holland, Italy, Germany, and many states in the US.

Due to environmental pollution by phosphates, manufacturers turned to phosphate substitutes. The principal substitutes were **EDTA** and **NTA**, neither of which are **biodegradable**, both form soluble compounds with heavy metals already present in water such as **lead** and **cadmium**. These compounds then reenter the water supply and are taken up by fish. EDTA is still used in some brands of laundry powder, but, increasingly, manufacturers are turning to substitutes such as **zeolites**. These silicate-based crystals soften water and are not thought to harm the environment. Zeolites are used in phosphate-free brands of laundry powder that are **biodegradable**. See also **Laundry powder**.

**Phosphoric acid** A corrosive, toxic, and powerfully irritant chemical, phosphoric acid is used as a rust remover. It emits toxic fumes when heated. Wear gloves if you are using this product and keep it away from your eyes and off your skin. Ensure that the area you are working in is well ventilated.

**Photocopier** Photocopiers can give off low levels of **carbon monoxide** and **ozone**. Keep photocopiers in a separate, well-ventilated space.

**Photodegradable** Substances that are photodegradable disintegrate when they are exposed to daylight. Certain types of photodegradable **plastic** have been developed for use in shopping bags.

**Photovoltaic cells** These cells collect solar energy and are used in **solar panels** for supplying heat and power to the home, as well as in solar-powered **calculators**. With such calculators **batteries** are unnecessary.

**Pigments** These are substances that give color, opacity, and consistency to **paint**. Most modern pigments are of mineral origin. Warm earth tones include red and yellow ochre, while brighter colors come from metal ores. White pigment was formerly made from white **lead**; now it is based on **titanium dioxide**. Pigments for coloring **fabrics**

were also used for paint. **Organic paint** suppliers stock mineral- and earth-derived pigments that you can mix with wall paint to create your own colors. For children's play and for educational use, paints colored with pure plant extracts, such as saffron crocus and madder, are also available from these suppliers.

**Pine** A fast-growing **softwood** grown in Europe, the UK, and North America. Pine is used for construction, furniture, joinery, and **wood** pulp for **paper**. It is a good, durable alternative to **tropical hardwoods** and is a **sustainable timber**. See the list of sustainable timber on p. 155.

**Pine**
**Pipes**
**Plaster**
**Plastic**

**Pipes** Many older houses still have some **lead** pipes, especially the pipe that connects the house to the **water** mains. Lead from pipes can leach into drinking water where it is a serious health risk, especially for children. Ask the local water authority to check lead levels in your tap water, especially in soft water areas where the risk of lead contamination is higher. Consider replacing pipes, but if this is not feasible invest in a **water filter** to reduce lead content, and always run the cold tap for a few minutes in the morning to clear water that has been standing overnight in pipes. Copper pipes are preferable to lead pipes, but make certain that lead-free solder is used for joints. (The EPA currently requires it for new and federally financed construction.) **Plastic** pipes are also used, but volatile chemical constituents from such plastics as **PVC** are likely to contaminate drinking water. Take the same precautions as for lead.

**Plaster** The two most common types of plaster are lime plaster and plaster of paris. Lime plaster is made of slaked lime, coarse sand, water, and fibrous material for binding. Plaster of paris is used for interior plasterwork and is made from **gypsum**, a naturally occurring mineral. Gypsum plasterboard is also used for ceilings. Plaster is a natural, nontoxic material that can be left unpainted. If you do paint over it, consider using **organic paint** to enable the plaster surfaces to "breathe". Avoid plaster products made from phosphogypsum, as these may harbor **radon**.

**Plastic** In the US around 35 percent of all the **packaging** used is made of plastic, and there are more than 50 kinds of plastic, 30 of them currently in everyday use. Plastic is a long-lasting material derived from oil, a nonrenewable resource that is in short supply. It is inappropriate, therefore, to simply throw it away. About 772,000 tons of plastic – representing 7 percent of US household **waste** by weight – are, however, disposed of each year. From an environmental point of view, some foamed **polystyrene**, a plastic used for such packaging as fast food containers and egg cartons, poses problems since it may still contain **CFC** foaming agents that damage the **ozone** layer. In addition, the plastic packaging materials currently available are not fully **biodegradable** and, because most packaging is composed of a mixture of plastics, it is difficult to sort and recycle. In the US and Sweden, a simple coding process identifies the six main types of plastic used in packaging. In Denmark, plastic bottles have been banned altogether, while in Germany, companies manufacturing plastic bottles are obliged to recycle those sold through supermarkets and stores. Each bottle carries a deposit that is refunded to the customer when it is returned.

**Plastic
(continued)**

Once in the environment, plastic doesn't degrade and claims the lives of many animals, birds, and fish, who become entangled in, or swallow, plastic bags and choke. Many are also strangled when entangled in the plastic rings on six-packs of canned beer and soft drinks. When 300 miles of Texas shoreline were cleaned up at the end of 1989, 15,600 plastic six-pack beer rings were picked up in just three hours. There are, however, two types of plastic used in bags ecolyte and bioplastic – that do biodegrade to some extent. Ecolyte is **photodegradable**: certain components in the plastic decompose in daylight, allowing the plastic to break up into small pieces. If it is buried in a landfill where sufficient daylight cannot reach it, the process is halted. Bioplastic, on the other hand, must be buried in order for certain components in the plastic to decompose. As with ecolyte, plastic pieces remain in the environment once the biodegradable element has gone. A trash bag made from recycled black plastic, has recently been developed that breaks down into a plastic dust within 12 months and leaves no trace after 10 years. Meanwhile, a fully-biodegradable plastic made from sugar has been developed in the UK and is being used to package a hair-care product. Using biodegradable plastic for consumer goods, however, does not have the full support

The living room is often a space for talking, reading, and relaxing, with an emphasis on comfortable furniture and soft **lighting**. Unfortunately the synthetic **carpet** and furnishing **fabrics**, **chipboard** fixtures, and **vinyl** wallcoverings common to many living rooms are not healthy materials. **TVs**, videos, stereos, and other electrical appliances combine with synthetic furnishings to cause static build up, and chemical sprays designed to scent and freshen air, succeed only in polluting it.

**Fire** Open fires, **gas**, solid fuel, or **wood**-burning stoves give out **combustion gases**. If there is insufficient **ventilation** in the room these polluting gases will be drawn into the room and will contaminate indoor air. Open fires are inefficient in terms of the **energy** they produce: as much as 80 percent of the heat generated can be lost up the chimney. If you have a fire in your home, be sure that your fireplace or stove is well constructed and maintained and have chimneys regularly swept. To reduce atmospheric pollution, always burn smokeless fuel. If you are contemplating buying or replacing a stove, consider a high-performance, clean-burning model. These modern woodstoves have advanced combustion systems, sometimes called "catalytic" burners, that reduce emissions of the pollutants in smoke and achieve up to 25 percent more efficiency than standard models.

1 Solid fuel stove
2 Essential oil burner
3 Ionizer
4 Window for ventilation and light
5 Floor cushions
6 Natural fabrics
7 Cotton or wool rug
8 Bowl of water
9 Pot-pourri
10 Solid wood fittings
11 House plants
12 Organic paint
13 Cane or wicker furniture
14 Fire-retardant fabric

**Upholstered furniture** Modern upholstered furniture may be stuffed with **polyurethane foam**, a serious fire hazard. New upholstered furniture in the US must, by law, contain a safer, modified foam, plus a **fire-retardant** covering fabric. Soft, upholstered furniture may also contribute to back problems, since it offers very little support for the lower back. Consider a low form of seating such as a natural **wool**- or **cotton**-filled **futon** sofa-bed; or try wicker and **cane** furniture; furniture made from solid **wood** with less padding that is designed to support the back; and floor cushions for sitting cross-legged – a posture that encourages relaxed breathing and a straight spine.

## Carpet and furnishings

Synthetic carpet and furnishings made from such fabrics as **acrylic** and **polyester** have been treated with **formaldehyde**, **insecticides**, and **fungicides**. Formaldehyde releases harmful vapors and is a suspected carcinogen, while insecticides and fungicides can cause irritations. Synthetics also cause static build up. Before use, always launder new covers and curtains, and steam clean carpets with plain water, to remove chemical residues. For cleaner, indoor air, and to reduce static, choose natural fabrics. Increasing humidity levels with **house plants** and bowls of **water** is another effective way to prevent static build up and improve the indoor climate.

**TV, video, and stereo** All these electrical appliances generate **electromagnetic fields (EMFs)**, electromagnetic radiation, static, and increase the proportion of positive ions, a situation that can by overcome by using an **ionizer** to raise the level of beneficial negative ions in the room.

**Paint and wallpaper** Synthetic **petrochemical** paint and vinyl wallpaper contain **plastic**, **solvents**, and **fungicides**. A healthier alternative is **organic paint** made from plant oils, resins, and binders. Organic paint contains no nonrenewable petrochemical derivatives and is nontoxic. And by letting air and moisture through, it helps the building to breathe.

**Living room**

of environmentalists, since it only serves to perpetuate a "throw-away mentality". Recycling and reusing are preferred options for plastic.

From a health perspective, **PVC** has given cause for concern since the raw material from which it is made, **vinyl chloride monomer**, is a carcinogen. The plasticizers used in this type of plastic are not chemically bound to the plastic and can be detached by coming into contact with oil or heat. Plasticizers in **clingfilm** food wrapping, for example, may contaminate food, especially if the food is warm or fatty. See individual entries for types of plastic.

### Steps you can take to reduce plastic usage
- Don't use plastic carrier bags when shopping. Save the bags you already have and take them with you, or take a more durable canvas or string shopping bag.
- Avoid overpackaged products: you are paying for the extra packaging. Buy fruit and vegetables loose rather than prepacked varieties.
- Choose **glass** bottles rather than plastic.
- Choose cardboard containers for eggs and canned drinks that are packaged together with cardboard rather than plastic rings. If no cardboard drinks packs are available, snip the plastic rings before throwing them away.
- Buy such products as drinks, oils, shampoo, and other cosmetics in shops where a refill service is offered.
- Reuse plastic containers for storage purposes, and use them for raising plant seedlings or cuttings.
- Choose black plastic trash bags made from recycled plastic, or try strong **paper** trash sacks.

**Plywood** This laminated **board** is commonly used in the home for some items of furniture and fixtures. The process of manufacturing plywood uses **formaldehyde** resin as a binder. Once in the home, and especially when new, formaldehyde can **outgas**. Always seal plywood fixtures with a nontoxic **paint** or **varnish**; look for "low emission" varieties of plywood; and consider using a solid **softwood**, such as **pine**.

**Polish, floor and furniture** Most **aerosol** polishes contain **silicone**, a **plastic**. They give furniture a shine but do not nourish or preserve **wood**. A few aerosols may still contain **CFCs** or other propellants that damage the **ozone** layer.

**Plywood**
**Polish, floor and furniture**

Most varieties contain **solvents**: these leave an unpleasant surface residue. Choose natural **beeswax** polish to protect and preserve your furniture, or make your own by melting together 2 oz beeswax, 5 fl oz real **turpentine**, and 2 tbsp pure **linseed oil**. Natural liquid polishes can be made by mixing 3 parts olive oil and 1 part white **vinegar**; or 2 parts vegetable oil with 1 part lemon juice; or 2 parts pure linseed oil and 1 part real turpentine. Apply all these polishes sparingly with a soft cloth. For oak, boil 2 pints beer with 1 tbsp sugar and 2 tbsp beeswax; cool, then apply with a soft cloth and allow to dry. Finish off with a chamois leather. Leather furniture can also be cleaned with a mixture of 1 cup vinegar and 1 cup pure linseed oil. If, however, you run out of polish or do not have the ingredients to hand, apply plain mayonnaise to wood furniture and wipe off. For wood floors, choose pure beeswax or carnauba wax polish. For **linoleum**, try a liquid floor soap with added **essential oil**, available from suppliers of **biodegradable** cleaning products.

**Polyalkylene glycol ethers** This group of chemicals is commonly found in **brake and clutch fluid**. They may irritate the skin and eyes. Take used or left over fluid to your local reclamation center or service station for disposal.

**Polycarbonate** A **plastic** used for **windows** and skylights, especially in mobile homes and greenhouses. Polycarbonate, unlike standard window **glass**, allows ultraviolet (UV) rays from the sun to pass through it. In summer, avoid over-exposure to UV and possible sunburn by limiting the amount of time you spend sitting beneath skylights or by windows made from polycarbonate. Furnishings beneath polycarbonate windows can also deteriorate due to UV penetration, and synthetic materials can give off unpleasant vapors. Ensure that there is adequate **ventilation** in areas with polycarbonate windows, and choose furnishings made from natural materials.

**Polychlorinated biphenyls** See **PCBs**.

**Poly-cotton blends** This mixture of **polyester** and **cotton** is commonly used for sheets and clothing. See **Polyester**.

**Polyester** This soft type of **plastic** is one of the most popular synthetic **fabrics**. It is commonly used for clothing, for bed linen, for **carpeting**, and for stuffing **duvets**. It is also found in mixtures with such natural fabrics as **cotton**, known as **poly-cotton blends**. The dyes in polyester fibers can cause skin irritation, and virtually all poly-cotton has been treated with a **formaldehyde** finish. Since polyester is a plastic, it does not readily absorb moisture, so it leaves you feeling sticky in warmer weather. In cold weather, polyester's poor thermal qualities mean that it retains very little of your body heat. Choose instead such natural fabrics as **cotton**, cotton flannel, and **wool**.

**Polyethylene** A **plastic** widely used for **packaging**, polyethylene comes in two varieties, high density **(HDPE)** and low density (LDPE). HDPE's uses include **bottles** for such household cleaners as **disinfectant** and **bleach**, and pharmaceutical containers. It is estimated that 2750 tons of HDPE are recycled by the plastic-reprocessing industry each year. LDPE is similar to **polythene** and is made into bags, sacks, trash liners, and bottles for **dishwashing liquid**.

**Polyethylene terephthalate (PET)** Of all the **plastics** used for packaging, PET presents the best option for **recycling**. It is widely used for soft drinks and carbonated **water**. Recycling 1 billion **bottles** every year would save 5500 tons of plastic. PET recycling programs are widely scattered in the US, although the plastics industry is now using a labeling code that should help to standardize the practice. Recycling plastic to make containers for food and drink is not viable: recycled plastic is likely to allow potentially harmful substances from the plastic to migrate into the foodstuffs.

**Polypropylene** This **plastic** is used for **packaging** such foods as margarine, biscuits, and crackers. A small percentage of the total production is recycled by the plastic processing industry annually. Polypropylene can be spun into tough fibers and is also used for nets and twine. It gives off toxic fumes when burned.

**Polystyrene** There are two types of polystyrene, a **plastic** with a variety of uses. Solid or crystal polystyrene is one type, and it is used to make such products as deli and yogurt containers and bottle caps. The other type is foamed polystyrene, commonly used for egg cartons, fast-food trays, disposable cups, protective packaging for fragile electronic equipment, and home **insulation**. Polystyrene gives off toxic fumes when burned. Expanded polystyrene may still contain **CFCs**, although there have been efforts by the foam plastics industry to use CFCs with the lowest ozone-damaging potential, or to replace it with pentane and **butane**. Extruded polystyrene, more commonly used for insulation, uses CFCs, but again, efforts are being made to curtail or eliminate their use altogether. See **Insulation** and **Packaging**.

**Polythene** See **Polyethylene**.

**Polythene**
**Polyurethane**
**Polyurethane foam**

**Polyurethane** Polyurethane belongs to the urethane group of synthetic resins that have a wide variety of applications, including **adhesives**, **paint**, **varnish**, and **plastic**. The manufacture of polyurethane can produce toxic **phosgene** gas, and polyurethane causes cancer in laboratory animals. It is, however, unlikely that you would absorb harmful amounts of this substance while using products containing it. The main health hazard presented by polyurethane occurs when it is in the form of **polyurethane foam**.

**Polyurethane foam** This substance has been used to upholster furniture since 1950, and it is a serious fire hazard. One in three deaths caused by fire in the home is attributed to the polyurethane foam in furniture. It catches fire easily, burns extremely rapidly, and gives off dense, black smoke containing poisonous cyanides that cause suffocation. New upholstered furniture sold in the US must, by law, contain a combustion-modified foam that ignites and burns less rapidly. Pre-1950 furniture will not contain polyurethane foam, but you can take safety precautions with any upholstered furniture made after that date by covering it with a **flameproof** fabric. Replace this type of foam as soon as you can with alternative fillings of natural fibers or combustion-modified foam.

Polyurethane foam is also used as an **insulation** material in the construction industry, and **CFCs** are used in its manufacture. Many companies, however, are responding to pressure from environmental groups and phasing out this environmentally-damaging foam insulation.

**Polyvinyl acetate (PVA)** PVA is a component of water-based **adhesives** and is of low toxicity.

**Polyvinyl chloride** See **PVC**.

**Poplar** Poplar is a temperate **hardwood** and a **sustainable timber**. Used for shelving, interior joinery, and turnery, it is tough and lightweight. See the list on p. 155.

**Pot-pourri** Pot-pourri is a mixture of dried flowers, **herbs**, and spices in various combinations, that, when placed on open containers, gives a sweet, fresh smell to your home. A natural and safe alternative to chemical **air freshener** that may deaden your sense of smell, pot-pourri mixtures are widely available and are suitable for any room in the house. You can also make up your own pot-pourri mix with flowers and herbs that you have grown and dried yourself, or buy them ready dried. Layer flowers and herbs alternately in jars with half a teaspoon of coarse salt and half a teaspoon of orris root powder (available from herbalists) sprinkled over each layer. Seal the jars and leave them in a dark place for three weeks. After this time, tip out the contents, mix with one or two teaspoons of an **essential oil** of your choice, stir, and put into bowls. If, after a time, the scent of the pot-pourri seems to be fading, add two or three more drops of essential oil.

**Pressed wood products** See **Board**.

**Pressure cooker** This piece of kitchen equipment cooks food rapidly by increasing air pressure and raising temperature. As well as saving **energy**, pressure cooking also conserves more of the nutrients in your food than conventional cooking. Choose pressure cookers made from stainless steel rather than **aluminum**. Unlike aluminum, stainless-steel surfaces will not break down when you cook acidic foods such as tomatoes.

**Primer** Used to prepare and seal **wood** and metal surfaces before painting, primers ensure that when **paint** is applied, it adheres. Primers formerly used white **lead** as a drying agent, but it is no longer found in products sold for DIY use. Most primers are oil-based and contain such **solvents** as **xylene**, plus **fungicides**. Primers for exterior wood that are labeled "preservative primers" may also contain such fungicides as **dichlofluanid** and **zinc naphthenate**. Protect your skin from primers, since they are irritants, and do not inhale the harmful solvent vapors. Take precautions against fire by keeping primers away from sources of ignition. Primers are highly flammable so never smoke when using them. Safer, solvent- and synthetic fungicide-free primers for wood and metal are available from **organic paint** suppliers.

**Propane** Propane gas is used in **bottled gas heaters**. It may also be used for heating and cooking in areas without supplies of natural **gas**. Propane gives off such **combustion gases** as **carbon dioxide** which can cause drowsiness or even suffocation in confined spaces. Make sure that bottled gas heaters are only used in well-ventilated spaces. Adequate ventilation will also protect against any **condensation** produced. Propane is highly flammable, so keep cylinders away from sources of ignition and have heaters regularly serviced.

Propane
Propane torch
Propylene glycol
Pump-action
spray

**Propane torch** Although a speedy way to remove **paint**, a propane torch is not, however, recommended for stripping off old paint. If the paint contains **lead** toxic fumes and tiny lead particles will be released. And unless you are experienced with a blow lamp, this method often results in scorched **wood**. Choose a water-based **paint stripper** instead: this type contains no harmful **solvents**.

**Propylene glycol** Commonly found in **antifreeze**. Propylene glycol, in common with many **solvents**, is irritating to the skin and eyes. Keep this product off your skin and always wash your hands after using it. Be certain, also, that antifreeze is not accessible to children: it tastes sweet but is toxic if swallowed.

**Pump-action spray** The pump-action spray contains no harmful **CFC** or other **ozone**-destroying propellants. It is, therefore, an environmentally sound alternative to **aerosols**. Many household and personal-care products are now available in pump-action sprays.

**PVA** See **Polyvinyl acetate**.

**PVC** Polyvinyl chloride, a versatile **plastic**, which has many uses from food **packaging** to **pipes** and credit cards. The raw material from which PVC is made, **vinyl chloride monomer**, is a known carcinogen and a powerful irritant. PVC is also used in some brands of **clingfilm** food wrapping. Fears about the monomer or the plasticizers in PVC migrating into foods and warm foods have led to the manufacture of plasticizer-free, or non-PVC, varieties. In Italy clingfilm may not be used to package such fatty foods as cheese and meat. In **pipes**, traces of plastic may contaminate **water** supplies. If you are worried about this, use a **water filter**. Never burn PVC; unless PVC is burned professionally in high-temperature incinerators it gives off toxic substances including **dioxins** and **phosgene** gas.

**Pyrethrins** These **insecticides** are the synthetic derivatives of the plant-based insecticide pyrethrum, and are used in **wood preservative**. Known also as pyrethroids, these compounds are powerful skin irritants and are suspected of causing damage to the peripheral nervous system. The pyrethroid group includes **permethrin**. See **Wood preservative** for alternatives.

**Pyrethroids** See **Pyrethrin**.

**Quaternary ammonium compounds** A group of nitrogen-based chemicals, that are commonly used as **fungicides** in exterior masonry **paint** and **wallpaper paste**. People with sensitive skin may find products containing these compounds irritating. Take precautions by protecting your skin and keeping them away from your eyes.

**Radon** A colorless, odorless, radioactive gas. Radon is formed by the decay of uranium, and is found in areas of predominantly granite rock, such as the Appalachian mountain chain. Radon gas seeps into houses from the rock and soil beneath, and from groundwater supplies that pass through radon-rich rock to be piped into homes. It then breaks down, emitting tiny particles that can seriously damage lung tissue. Radon has also been linked with leukemia, skin and kidney cancers, and some childhood cancers. According to estimates from the Environmental Protection Agency, 20,000 people die each year from lung cancer brought on by radon exposure, and the EPA puts the number of homes with radon levels above the government's "action level" at more than 10 million. Radon rises through the subsoil and can enter through cracks in the building structure. It is nine times heavier than air so it tends to collect in the **basement** (p. 50), or in the lowest part of the house if there is no basement. Radon from groundwater supplies finds its way into tap water and can concentrate in the **bathroom** (p. 80) where the vapor may be released from the **shower** in a fine spray. Radon exposure via showers constitutes a particular health risk since in this form it is most easily absorbed by the lungs. According to a Canadian study, radon levels increased rapidly during a short, warm shower, and the gas did not disperse until 90 minutes later.

### Action
- Contact your local state or federal EPA office for information on radon testing. Currently, over 200 firms have been qualified by the federal agency to test for radon levels in the home. Grants or low-interest loans may be available to radon-proof homes that are above the to check radon levels in your home "action level" of four picocuries per liter of air (pCi/L).
- Ensure that your basement has good through-**ventilation**, and that the crawl space under suspended floors is also well ventilated. You can also consider installing a fan or use vents or airbricks.
- Seal cracks in solid floors, walls, and suspended floors, and gaps around service **pipes**. Cover suspended floors with heavy **polythene** sheeting and lay wooden floor boards on top.
- Open a window while showering and make sure the bathroom has a good supply of fresh air by installing vents in the walls.
- If you are concerned about radon in drinking water, install an in-line **water filter**. It is claimed that one type can significantly reduce radon levels.
- Smokers, or those who live with smokers, are at particular risk in the presence of radon. Recent information indicates that radon may have a synergistic effect with cigarette smoke, more than doubling the risk of cancer.

**Ramin**
**Rat and mouse poison**

**Ramin** This is a **tropical hardwood** and an endangered **timber**. Malaysia is the main supplier of ramin. Avoid products made from this timber: destruction of valuable rainforest has been particularly widespread in Malaysia. Choose, instead, from the range of **sustainable timber** listed on p. 155.

**Rat and mouse poison** Chemicals designed to kill rats and mice, called rodenticides, are highly toxic to humans if accidentally swallowed or inhaled. These chemicals act as anticoagulants: they prevent blood from clotting, and so the rodents die from internal bleeding. Many rodents, however, have developed a resistance to certain types of poison, notably **warfarin**. Stronger substances are now used that must be kept well away from children and pets. Anticoagulant poisons also pose a serious hazard to haemophiliacs. A single dose of such poisons kills rodents, but they may take up to three weeks to die. During this time, and after, they may be picked up by pets, or owls and other birds of prey, and they will be poisoned in turn. Keep your kitchen clean, and all food covered, to discourage rats and mice. If they persist in getting in, use a mouse or rat trap from time to time, or get a cat. If you prefer not to kill rodents, try a humane trap. These devices catch rodents without harming them. You then release them outside. They may, of course, pay a return visit.

**Rattan**
**Rayon**
**Recycling**

**Rattan** A palm used to make cane furniture, basketware, and mats. Most rattan grows in the rainforests of Southeast Asia. Excessive exploitation of these forests and widespread land clearing has, however, resulted in a shortage of rattan supplies in Thailand and the Philippines. Whenever possible buy rattan products from suppliers who import rattan from managed plantations, and from ethical traders who guarantee fair wages and equitable conditions in the country of origin.

**Rayon** Manufactured from natural **cellulose** found in wood and plant pulp, rayon is a synthetic fiber that may be treated to prevent it from creasing. It is often mixed with **cotton** and used in **sanitary protection products**. These may have been whitened with **chlorine bleach**, so look for cotton/rayon products that are unbleached or made from pulp that has been treated with an **oxygen bleach**. Rayon is largely derived from eucalyptus trees. These trees soak up a tremendous amount of water from the soil, and may cause shortages in local supplies for drinking, as was the case in Northern Sumatra.

**Recycling** Americans produce about 154 tons of domestic **waste** each year. Although it has been estimated that around 50 percent of recyclable domestic waste could, in fact, be recycled, only 11 percent actually is. Waste disposal is expensive. In small, densely populated countries such as the UK and Denmark, landfill sites for dumping waste are becoming scarce and their increasingly-distant locations mean higher transport costs. In the US, about half the cities have exhausted their landfill space as of 1990. Separating and recycling as much of your waste as possible is an effective way to slow down the waste disposal problem. Recycling also means we use less of the earth's already depleted natural resources, while making products from recycled materials uses considerably less **energy** and causes less pollution than extracting and processing raw materials. Making **cans** from recycled **aluminum**, for example, takes 96 percent less energy than making them from raw bauxite ore. You can also help to save both energy and trees by choosing recycled **paper** products including toilet paper, stationery, and kitchen towels. Buying furniture made from recycled lumber and second-hand solid **wood** furniture also reduces the vast numbers of trees cut down each year.

**Recycling (continued)**

Recycling begins at home. The initial separation of waste in the home constitutes the first step toward successful recycling. In such European countries as Austria, separate bins are provided for sorting out waste, while in New York State, strict laws encourage the separation of domestic rubbish. In Sheffield, designated the UK's first Recycling City, some householders are provided with a blue box that has separate compartments for storing different recyclable materials. Based on a scheme run in Ontario, Canada, a weekly door-to-door collection of these blue boxes by a purpose-built vehicle makes recycling easy, especially for elderly people and those without cars. Within your own community, you can work for recycling centers to be set up in your area by approaching your local government, environmental groups, and managers of large supermarkets. Then organize a waste-separation center in your **kitchen** (p. 16) or wherever you have the appropriate space. Start with four containers: one for **glass** (you'll have to separate it later into clear, brown- and green-colored bottles); one for aluminum – cans, foil, and pie plates; one for steel cans; and one for paper. If you have a garden, keep a bucket for leftover food, and fruit and vegetable peelings, and put them on the compost heap. You can also recycle textiles and reuse **plastics** if plastic recycling programs have not yet been established in your community.

## Glass

In the US, more than 28 billion glass containers are thrown away each year; only 11 percent are recycled. In Germany 37 percent of glass is recycled and in Holland, 67 percent. Always take back glass **bottles**, such as milk bottles, that are returnable, as well as those bottles that have a deposit. Store remaining glass bottles and jars in a cardboard box; rinse them and remove the metal tops, and take them to your nearest **bottle bank**, or reclamation center. Glass can effectively be recycled over and over again.

## Aluminum

Rinse aluminum cans, open both ends, crush them (by stamping on them, but wear stout boots) to save space, store, and then take them to your nearest can collection center. Many soft drinks cans are made from aluminum, but if you are in doubt as to a can's composition hold a magnet to it. Magnets will not stick to aluminum cans. Aluminum foil and foil food trays are also accepted by some charitable organizations.

**Recycling (continued)**

## Steel

Many cans for human and pet food are made of steel, coated with tin, and magnets stick to them. Although not as valuable as aluminum, the steel can be recovered and recycled. In the US, only 5 percent of steel cans are recycled. Rinse and crush steel cans and take them to your nearest recycling center. Some facilities take both aluminum and steel cans then sort them later using powerful electromagnets.

## Paper

Around 29 percent of America's paper is currently recycled. Save newspapers, magazines, cards, junk mail, and wrapping paper, and take them to your nearest waste paper collection point. If you work at home, save used stationery and computer paper. This type of lightly-inked paper is particularly valuable and can be sold to waste paper merchants. If local merchants will take only large quantities, donate it to friends who work in offices where recycling programs are already established. Health and retirement centers may welcome magazines. Unfortunately if there is a glut of recycled paper the price it brings drops steeply. Stimulate demand for more recycled paper collections by buying recycled paper products. Making paper from recycled material uses between 30 and 55 percent less energy than processing virgin pulp and reduces related air pollution by over 90 percent.

### Textiles
Donate old clothes to thrift shops and charity sales. Rag merchants also collect garments for reprocessing. Their uses include felt and furniture stuffing. **Wool** and **cotton** garments may be unravelled and the thread respun.

### Metal
Take larger metal items and appliances to scrap-metal dealers for stripping and reclamation. They usually buy copper, **iron**, **lead**, steel, and **zinc**.

**Refrigerator, refrigerator-freezer**

### Plastics
Only recently has plastic in **packaging** been labelled according to the type used. Prior to this program, sorting and recycling was extremely difficult. Each American uses about 190 pounds of plastic each year - 60 pounds of it, or five million tons nationwide, is packaging. Trash bags made from recycled plastic are, however, available and one variety is said to be fully **biodegradable**. Cut down on the amount of plastic-packaged goods that you buy. Reuse such plastic containers as deli containers and margarine tubs for storing food, household and workshop objects, and for planting cuttings and seedlings. Consider buying cosmetics and bodycare products from suppliers that offer a refill service.

**Refrigerator**, **refrigerator-freezer** At present refrigerators still contain **CFCs** that damage the **ozone** layer and accelerate the **greenhouse effect**. Two of the most damaging CFCs, CFC 11 and 12, are commonly used in the insulating foam of standard models, and as coolants. Models are currently available, however, that use insulation with a 50 percent reduction in CFCs. Some use a different type of CFC that is less damaging to the ozone layer, HCFC 22. Insulation that does not contain CFCs has, however, been developed and we should be seeing a range of CFC-free refrigerators in the near future. In terms of **energy** consumption, refrigerators show more variation between models than any other appliance, and running a refrigerator can account for a large slice of your energy bill. In the US, for example, one-third of the average household energy bill is attributable to refrigeration. A standard refrigerator uses 270 kWh of electricity a year, but the best available European model uses only 80 kWh a year. When buying a new refrigerator, choose an **energy efficient** model, or the most energy efficient of the CFC-free models when they become available. But do not simply throw out your old model as the CFCs escape into the atmosphere when old refrigerators are scrapped and broken up. Although those contained in the refrigerator insulation cannot be reclaimed, those used as coolants can be extracted with special equipment. The CFCs are then sealed in a cylinder, cleaned, and reused. Some local refrigeration contractors, retailers, and commercial companies offer this service.

To ensure maximum efficiency from your existing refrigerator, save energy by keeping the condenser – the coils at the back – clean and free from dust. A dirty condenser uses 30 percent more electricity. Check the door seal periodically for any leaks, keep it clean, and always shut it firmly to avoid wasting energy. Defrost your refrigerator regularly, and keep the freezer compartment clear of ice. A well-stocked refrigerator uses less power than a poorly-stocked one, since more energy is needed to cool empty space. Siting your refrigerator away from ovens and in a cool place is also more economical, and a refrigerator **thermometer** will make sure that you have the correct setting.

**Resins**

**Resins** Resins occur naturally in **wood** from **pine**, **spruce**, and other coniferous trees. Resins give off a sharp, distinctive scent; this resinous vapor is particularly strong when the **wood** is new and may be a source of irritation to sensitive people. You can overcome this problem by buying recycled wood, or furniture made from older wood, or sealing the surface with a nontoxic **varnish**.

Synthetic resins are also widely used as binders for varieties of **board**, including **chipboard** and **plywood**. **Formaldehyde** resin is commonly used, giving off harmful vapors, especially when the board is new. Use solid wood, "low-emission" boards where available, or seal any surfaces with a nontoxic varnish or **paint**.

**Rodenticides** This group of chemicals is designed to kill rats and mice. See **Rat and mouse poison**.

**Roofing material** Roofing felt, commonly used for flat roofs, consists of glass fiber or mineral fiber. This is then topped with a layer of thick **bitumen** mixed with sand and small stones, or with asphalt. Felt or corrugated roofing that contains **asbestos** may still be around, but asbestos-based roofing products have generally been phased out. Avoid any roofing product containing asbestos since the dangerous fibers will be released when the material is disturbed. Bitumen is a skin irritant so wear gloves when using it.

**Rosewood** An endangered **tropical hardwood**. Rosewood is also sometimes known as jacaranda. Avoid products made from rosewood and see the list of **sustainable timber** on p. 155 for alternatives.

**Rubber** The rubber tree, native to South America and Malaysia, is tapped for its **latex**. This sticky liquid is then processed under heat and pressure to give it more resilience and make it more elastic. Natural rubber was widely used as a **flooring** material but has now been largely replaced by **plastics**. Rubber sheeting is still available and is preferable to plastic for babies' cribs.

**Sanforized** This term is applied to **fabrics**, usually **cotton**, and indicates that the fabric has been preshrunk.

**Sanitary-protection products** In 1989 the UK Women's Environmental Network campaigned against the use of **paper** pulp bleached with **chlorine** in sanitary napkins and other sanitary products. The campaign centered on the possible contamination of sanitary products by **dioxins**. These toxic chemicals, formed as a by-product of the chlorine bleaching process, cause cancer. The chemical effluent discharged from paper mills is also a serious **water** pollutant. When the campaign attracted publicity, fears of dioxin contamination moved to disposable **diapers** and went on to embrace a range of paper products including coffee filters and tea bags. As a result, some manufacturers now offer a choice of bleached and unbleached sanitary products. Of the bleached varieties of napkins and tampons, the majority now contain viscose rayon, pulp, or **cotton** treated with less harmful **oxygen bleach**.

Sanitary products, according to the label, can be flushed down the **toilet**. This method of disposal, however, can pose health and environmental problems when storm water floods older municipal sewage systems and washes their contents into the oceans. Once in the water, they take around 120 days to break down but the **plastic** backing is not **biodegradable**. Put sanitary products in paper bags and dispose of them in the trash container. ▷

A less wasteful, less environmentally-damaging, and less expensive type of sanitary protection is now available from at least a half-dozen different manufacturers. It consists of a washable and reusable cotton towel, and it is estimated that 15 such towels will provide one woman with a year's supply of sanitary wear.

**Sapele** This is a **tropical hardwood**, is an endangered **timber.** Avoid products made from sapele unless you are satisfied that it comes from managed plantations. See the list of **sustainable timber** on p. 155 for alternatives.

Sapele
Scouring powder
Sealant
Selenium
sulphide

**Scouring powder** Many brands of scouring powder, or **abrasive cleaner**, contain **chlorine bleach**, a strong irritant that is environmentally damaging. Other varieties may contain **ammonia**. Never mix ammonia-based products with chlorine bleach; this releases potentially deadly chlorine gas. Most surface cleaners also contain **phosphates**, although not in large quantities. The harsh, abrasive action of scouring powders can also damage certain surfaces, especially fiberglass. Gentler cleaners for **bath**, sinks, and worktops that are nontoxic and effective, include **borax** and **bicarbonate of soda**. Borax has disinfecting and mild, bleaching properties. Sprinkle it on a damp cloth and use as you would a scouring powder. Bicarbonate of soda also works well: apply on a damp cloth as before. **Washing soda** cuts grease and is an excellent nontoxic cleaner for heavier jobs, such as floors and walls. **Biodegradable** cream cleaner is also available from supermarkets and health food stores. Based on finely-powdered chalk, this type of cleaner contains no bleach or synthetic perfume and does not pollute waterways.

**Sealant** Sealants can irritate the skin so treat them with caution. **Acrylic** types are generally not hazardous but **silicone** sealants, used for **bath** and sink surrounds, emit harmful fumes while drying. Manufacturers recommend application of these types in ventilated areas only. Open windows and try not to inhale the fumes. Once cured, this type of sealant poses no problems.

**Selenium sulphide** This ingredient of anti-dandruff shampoos is a suspected animal carcinogen and easily absorbed through the scalp. Avoid shampoos containing this powerful substance if you have broken or sensitive skin on your scalp. Try regular scalp massage, brushing well with a brush, or use a gentle herbal shampoo.

**Shampoo** Most shampoos on the market comply with legislation in terms of biodegradability, but some contain **formaldehyde**, a suspected carcinogen that is used as a preservative. Avoid dandruff shampoos based on **selenium sulphide**, a powerful irritant and a suspected animal carcinogen. Choose gentle herbal shampoos and opt for **cruelty-free** products if you are opposed to **animal testing**.

**Shellac** A natural resin obtained from tropical trees. Shellac is a fine lacquer that makes an excellent, nontoxic **varnish** for solid **wood** furniture. It will also seal in up to 80 percent of the fumes emitted by **chipboard** and **plywood**.

**Shower** Save **water** by showering rather than bathing. A **bath** uses more than twice as much water as a five-minute shower. Some showers are described as "power showers" although this may not mean a faster flow, only that the shower is pump assisted. High rates of flow can prove very expensive and consume a great deal of water: some power showers can pump out up to nine gallons of water a minute, and for these you may even need an extra water tank. A standard shower uses upwards of three gallons of water a minute, with the average five-minute shower using 15 gallons. To save water, consider fitting a shower with a low-flow head, and take shorter showers. To save **energy**, choose a shower with a built-in anti-scald control and turn down the thermostat on the water heater. The regular cleaning and descaling of shower heads also ensures more efficient operation.

**Sick building syndrome** This term describes a variety of symptoms that debilitate people working in some office and public buildings. Such symptoms, however, can also be experienced in the home. Conditions common to both, include **air conditioning** and sealed **windows** that cannot be opened to let in fresh air. Air conditioning is considered necessary to improve the indoor climate, but poorly-maintained systems can be harmful. Air ducts and vents must be regularly cleaned, or they become fouled with dirt and pollutants, and then recirculate them around the building.

Shampoo
Shellac
Shower
Sick building
syndrome

One estimate indicates that up to three-quarters of America's office buildings with air conditioning were "sick". Whether in office blocks or the **home office** (p. 176), heat, static and **electromagnetic fields** are generated by the electronic circuits in such equipment as **personal computers** and **photocopiers**. Electrical equipment may also generate **ozone**. Synthetic **carpeting** and **chipboard** furniture and fixtures add to the bad atmosphere by contaminating the air with harmful **formaldehyde** vapor.

Make certain that your home is well ventilated and that windows can be opened. **House plants**, especially spider plants, (*Chlorophytum elatum* var. *vittatum*) improve the indoor climate naturally by absorbing pollutants and helping to regulate moisture levels in the air. An **ionizer** balances the positive ions generated by electrical machinery with beneficial negative ions, and reduces static. Avoid pollution from formaldehyde by choosing natural materials such as solid **wood** for furniture, plus **wool** carpets or **cotton** rugs.

**Silicone** Silicones are used in oils, waxes, and types of **rubber**. In the home, bath **sealant** may be based on silicone. Avoid breathing in the vapor while this type of sealant is drying and open windows. Furniture **polish**, too, often contains silicone. This kind of polish will leave a residue that can eventually mar the surface of your furniture. For preference, use natural **beeswax** on solid **wood** surfaces.

**Silver polish** See **Metal polish**.

**Sink cleaner** See **Scouring powder**.

**Sisal** Native to South America, this cactus-like plant yields strong leaf fibers. Once the fibers reach a certain length they can be cleaned and fashioned into matting. Sisal mats make an excellent, hard-wearing floor covering for areas where durability is a priority.

**Size** This is a weak glue made from rabbit skins. Mix size with artists' **pigment** and **water** to make a subtle color wash for painting walls. Soak one cup of size in 2 pints of water overnight, heat in a *bain marie* (double boiler), then add one part pigment and five parts water. Mix well and use at once.

**Soda crystals** See **Washing soda**.

**Sodium hydrogensulphite** A common component of powdered **toilet cleaner**, this acidic substance produces dilute **sulphuric acid** when it mixes with the **water** in the **toilet** bowl. Even dilute sulphuric acid is a serious irritant, so take care not to breathe in the vapor from powdered toilet cleaners, and guard against splashing your eyes or skin. Never mix this type of acidic cleaner with **bleach** as poisonous **chlorine** gas will be released. See **Toilet cleaner** for safer alternatives.

**Sodium hydroxide** Commonly known as **caustic soda**, sodium hydroxide is a corrosive substance found in some varieties of **oven** and **drain cleaner**. Even in weak solutions, caustic soda is particularly hazardous to the eyes and can cause severe skin problems. It produces birth defects in laboratory animals and is toxic to fish. Do not mix cleaners containing this chemical with those that are **ammonia**-based: toxic ammonia gas will result. See **Drain cleaner** and **Oven cleaner** for safe alternatives.

**Sodium hypochlorite** The common active ingredient of **chlorine bleach**, sodium hypochlorite is a corrosive chemical that can cause skin burns if accidentally spilled. The fumes given off irritate the eyes and the respiratory system. Do not use this type of bleach if you have a septic tank as it will destroy the bacteria that break down sewage. Sodium hypochlorite is also toxic to fish and other forms of aquatic life. Never mix bleach with any other **toilet cleaner** as the ensuing chemical reaction produces poisonous **chlorine** gas.

**Sodium perborate** A type of **oxygen bleach** commonly found in **laundry powder**, sodium perborate does not need an added stabilizer to stop it from becoming activated while still in the packet, unlike **sodium percarbonate**. For this reason, some manufacturers of laundry powder prefer it. According to research in Germany in 1988, however, perborate bleach left behind residues that were considered potentially harmful to water plants. Sodium percarbonate, on the other hand, is not considered to be harmful to the environment. See **Laundry powder** for alternatives.

Babies and young children have a faster rate of respiration and digestion than adults. For their body size and weight, they take in greater quantities of air, food, and water. If these elements contain pollutants and toxins, babies and small children absorb proportionately more of them. It is essential, therefore, that the nursery is a healthy, safe environment.

**Paint** Vapors from **solvent**-based paint may cause respiratory problems in babies. Choose quick-drying, **lead**-free, water-based paint. Try using low-odor **emulsion paint** or **organic paint**.

**Bedding** Polyester and **cotton** mixtures, often known as **poly-cotton blends**, have been treated with **formaldehyde**, a suspected carcinogen. Choose instead cotton, and cotton flannel sheets. Always wash bed linen before first use. Cotton cellular blankets are comfortably light and they are a good choice for babies. Use natural, **rubber** undersheets.

**Carpeting and flooring** Most synthetic carpets have been treated with **fungicides** and formaldehyde. In preference to carpeting, choose natural **linoleum** or **cork** tiles with cotton or **wool** rugs.

**Crib and bed** Choose a smooth-edged crib with side bars spaced at intervals no greater than 1.5-2in. For preference, leave the crib unpainted and, if necessary, treat it with natu-

ral **varnish** or **beeswax**. Avoid metal-framed beds and sprung mattresses; these may become magnetized by the domestic electricity supply, creating **electromagnetic fields (EMFs)**. These fields are thought to interfere with the body's electrical impulses. Choose beds for children made from such **sustainable softwoods** as **pine**, with a slatted base. Team them with unsprung mattresses filled with cotton or wool.

**Diapers** Cotton, terry-towelling diapers have been largely superseded by the disposable variety. There are, however, many problems associated with disposable diapers. For example, they may be contaminated with carcinogenic **dioxin**

residues and the **plastic** linings
of most disposable diapers are
not **biodegradable**. Terry diapers are a safer alternative and
help to prevent diaper rash,
they also present no **waste**
disposal problems, although
washing them is time-consuming. If you prefer disposables,
choose varieties that have
biodegradable linings and have
not been bleached with **chlorine**. Reusable, washable, wool
diaper-covers are a good alternative to plastic pants.

**Electricity supply** Electrical
sockets at floor level pose a
potential safety risk unless
fitted with covers. Some specialists are also concerned
about the EMFs generated by
the domestic electricity supply.

To reduce EMFs, try using a
**neutralizing undersheet** and
consider installing a **demand
switch**, which cuts off the
electricity supply to the nursery at night.

**Baby-care products** Many commercial baby-care products
contain **petrochemicals** and
fragrances that can irritate
babies' respiratory systems
and skins. Choose instead
plant-based products.

**Toys** Choose solid wood toys
for young children, plus cuddly
toys made from cotton, wool,
and leather. If the wood is
painted, check that the paint
used is nontoxic. Reuse toys
by donating them to a library
or to a local playgroup.

**Nursery**

**Sodium percarbonate** This chemical has a mild, bleaching action and can be found in some types of **laundry powder** and **stain remover**. As an ingredient of laundry powders, it has to be stabilized by the addition of **EDTA**, a substance that causes water pollution, to stop it working while still in the packet. Packaged separately, it needs no stabilizer and it is the type of bleach preferred by one manufacturer of **biodegradable** washing powder for two reasons: first, it has no harmful effects on plant life, and second, it becomes active at a relatively low temperature, 104°F. Sodium percarbonate is an irritant substance so keep it away from your eyes and off your skin. See **Laundry powder** and **Stain remover** for alternatives.

Sodium
percarbonate
Softwoods
Solar heating

**Softwoods** The rather misleading terms softwood and **hardwood** refer to the cell-structure of trees not to the strength or durability of the timber. In general, softwoods include the conifers, and one of these, yew, is one of the hardest woods. Hardwoods include all the broadleafed trees, one of which, balsa, is also one of the softest timbers. Most imported hardwoods are from unsustainable sources, and a good portion of those come from tropical rainforests. Since tropical deforestation poses serious environmental problems on a global scale, alternatives to tropical hardwoods are essential. In many cases, softwoods can be substituted for hardwoods, as they have a wide variety of applications in the home. They are better suited to managed plantations and replanting schemes since, in general, they contain faster growing trees than hardwood species. Softwoods such as **pine** and **spruce** are, in fact, grown specifically for furniture, joinery and **paper** making. When trees in such plantations are felled, new seeds are planted to ensure forest continuity. See the list of **sustainable timber** on p. 155 for more softwoods.

**Solar heating** There are two types of solar heating methods: active or passive. Active solar heating utilizes such appliances as **solar panels**, usually inserted into a sun-facing roof. The heat absorbed by the panels is then stored in water tanks or slabs of rock under the floor, and distributed around the house by means of a fan- or pump-assisted network of pipes and ducts. Passive solar heating requires that the building itself is designed as a solar collector. This involves absorption of the sun's heat through large, double- or triple-glazed, sun-facing windows or conservatories. The building structure itself then allows retention of the heat and circulation through the house without the use of mechanical devices. In both systems, blinds are usually drawn over the glass during the day to prevent overheating in very hot weather, and at night to prevent the collected heat from escaping.

**Solar panels** Safe, clean, and with no moving parts, the latest designs in solar panels can cut your electricity bill for heating water by between 40 and 50 percent. Solar panels are made from an abundant material, silicone, and work by absorbing the sun's **energy**, even, to some extent, on cloudy days. To conserve daytime heat generated from solar panels, you will need to install water tanks or a rock bed to retain the heat and release it at night.

**Solder** See **Lead**.

**Solvents** These substances are capable of dissolving other materials to make them liquid. Widely used in a variety of DIY products, including **adhesives**, **paint**, **varnish**, and **stain remover**, solvents give off powerful, irritant fumes that are easily absorbed through the skin. Prolonged exposure to the solvent **1,1,1-trichloroethane (methylchloroform)** can damage the eyes. When inhaled, solvents can produce symptoms of drowsiness, dizziness, and euphoria, hence the practice of solvent abuse, which has proved fatal. In response to this problem, solvent-based adhesives have been taken off display in many DIY stores. Some solvents, notably 1,1,1-trichloroethane commonly found in **correction fluid**, are harmful to the environment since they contain **chlorine** compounds that deplete the **ozone** layer. It is estimated that 1,1,1-trichloroethane is responsible for 13 percent of the ozone-destroying chlorine compounds currently in the upper atmosphere. Long-term exposure to solvents has, in certain cases, resulted in liver and kidney disease. In August 1990 a UK survey of professional painters using solvent-based paint found that 93 percent showed symptoms of solvent poisoning, including nausea, headaches, and stomach, chest, and lung problems. The majority of solvents are highly flammable.

When using solvents, make sure that you open a window to help disperse the vapor. Always replace tops and caps immediately after use. Guard against spilling products containing solvents on your skin, and keep them away from sources of ignition including pilot lights and cigarettes. Avoid solvents whenever possible, choosing water-based varieties of such products as paint and adhesives instead. See individual entries.

**Sound insulation** Noise from neighbors above or below can be a problem in apartments converted from a single house. To insulate floors, take up the floorboards and put down a thick, mineral fiber blanket to make a "floating floor". See that the surface is absolutely flat then fasten floorboards to wooden nailers on top. For ceilings, use mineral fiber, nailers, and plasterboard. If you live by a noisy road, seal all cracks around windows and consider using storm windows or secondary glazing. Make sure, however, that you retain adequate **ventilation**. See also **Insulation materials**.

**Space heaters** An electric heater consumes electricity at a faster rate than either a **washing machine** or a **tumble dryer**. A **bottled gas heater** is only slightly less expensive to run. It is generally accepted that, for heating a room there is little difference in cost between **gas** wall heaters, gas radiant or convection heaters, and most forms of **central heating**. Natural gas is, however, more cost-efficient than electricity and causes less pollution. A fuel-burning stove is more efficient than an open fire. See **Bottled gas heaters**, **Central heating**, **Energy saving**, and **Insulation**, for further information.

**Spruce** This fast-growing **softwood** is grown in North America. It is a **sustainable timber** and used for construction and joinery. See the list on p. 155.

**Stain remover** Many brands of stain remover contain such irritant substances as **sodium percarbonate**, and spot removers for grease contain the harmful solvent **1,1,1-trichloroethane**. Stain removers are hazardous if accidentally splashed in the eyes or on the skin, and manufacturers warn against inhaling the vapor. Those without child-proof tops should be kept well away from children. Stain removers are also flammable. For safer and nontoxic stain removal, try the following: **borax** (one part borax to eight parts water) for blood, urine, coffee and tea, mold, and chocolate stains; salt or soda water for wine stains; **washing soda** for blood, fruit juice, tea and coffee, and for removing chewing gum; for ink stains mix together 1 tbsp white **vinegar**, 1 tbsp milk, 1 tbsp lemon juice, and 1 tsp borax; for grass stains – rub on glycerine (glycerol) before washing; try eucalyptus oil for tar, oil, and grass stains – rub in well before washing, adding washing soda to remove the grease; to remove perspiration stains add half a cup of **bicarbonate of soda** or white **vinegar** to water for soaking, before washing.

**Stationery** Save trees by using both sides of the writing **paper**. Buy recycled stationery products. A wide range is available, including paper, envelopes, greeting cards, computer stationery, reusable labels, and personal organizer refills. See also **Paper**.

**Steam iron cleaner** See **Descaler**.

**Stoves Gas** stoves use up to two-thirds less **energy** than electric models with quick warm-up times and instant heat control on the burners. Electric grills, in particular, require longer pre heating before food can be cooked, and the insulation around grills on some stoves has been found to be poor. Gas production also results in less **carbon dioxide** and less environmental pollution than electricity production. Choose a gas stove with automatic ignition which, according to the US Gas Research Institute, cuts fuel consumption and emissions of **combustion gases** by one-third. Another energy-efficiency indicator is the amount of oven **insulation** and some cookers offer a slow cook setting on the oven for greater economy. To save energy when cooking, use the oven only if you have more than one dish to cook. A full oven is more **energy efficient**. Choose pans that cover the burner ring and avoid wasting gas by keeping the flame under the pan, not up the sides. Always put lids on saucepans and use as little **water** as possible. This saves energy and reduces the amount of **condensation** in the **kitchen** (p. 16). You can also save energy by investing in a layered steamer to cook different types of vegetables. This method needs only one burner and conserves essential nutrients. A **pressure cooker** is also an excellent energy-saving device for healthy cooking that conserves vital nutrients. Install a **stove hood** vented to the outside, and always use it when you cook to help reduce condensation, and smells.

**Stove hood** A hood fitted over your stove must be vented to the outside. It will absorb **combustion gases**, reduce smells, and help reduce **condensation**. For best results, combine a stove hood with an **extractor fan**. Some stove hoods already have a filtering device and these will not therefore require venting.

**Styrene** Used in two-part **filler**, styrene is a **solvent** that can irritate the skin. Exposure to high concentrations of this substance has resulted in serious eye injuries, while long-term exposure is associated with damage to the central nervous system. Although using filler containing styrene for DIY jobs about the home is unlikely to result in toxic levels of vapor, take precautions by ensuring that there is plenty of **ventilation**, and protect your skin and eyes. **Acrylic** and **cellulose** varieties of filler are safer.

**Sulphamic acid** Commonly found in **descaler** for kettles, sulphamic acid is an irritant to the eyes and the skin. See **Descaler** for safer alternatives.

**Sulphur dioxide** This polluting gas emitted by **coal**-fired power stations, is the biggest contributor to **acid rain**. However, efforts are being made world-wide to clean up such emissions. Most of the reductions will be achieved by using or importing low-sulphur coal and fitting scrubbing devices (Flue Gas Desulphurization), to power station and factory chimneys. These devices are already in place in factories around the world. See also **Energy**.

**Sulphuric acid** Used as a car battery acid, sulphuric acid is a powerful and highly corrosive substance. Protect your eyes and hands when handling car batteries: sulphuric acid will burn the skin, and continued exposure may cause dermatitis. Do not handle the powder that collects around battery terminals as this is also toxic. Sulphuric acid may be produced, also, when powdered **toilet cleaner** based on **sodium hydrogensulphate** mixes with water in the **toilet**. See **Toilet cleaner** for safer alternatives.

    **Acid rain**, a major environmental threat, is produced

mainly when the **sulphur dioxide**, emitted primarily by **coal**-burning power stations and by other plants burning coal, oil, or **gas**, combines with **nitrogen oxides** and water vapor in the atmosphere to form dilute sulphuric acid.

**Surfactants** Found in **laundry powder**, surfactants are synthetic cleaning agents that separate out the dirt. Soap was formerly used as a surfactant until scum became a problem in hard-**water** areas. Manufacturers then changed to synthetics, but the first types caused excessive foam in rivers and sewage farms. The majority of surfactants today are made from **petrochemicals** that are 90 percent **biodegradable**. Those used by the makers of biodegradable cleaning products, however, are based on such plant oils as coconut, palm, and **linseed**, and these are 100 percent biodegradable. See also **Laundry powder**.

**Sustainable** This term has a wide range of applications in the environmental movement. Sustainable processes and materials ideally fulfil several criteria. Generally speaking, materials come from resources that are renewable, and not from those that are being depleted or are endangered. The manufacture, use, and disposal of sustainable materials does not cause unnecessary damage to the environment, nor does it consume excessive amounts of **energy** or result in unsatisfactory quantities of **waste**. Finally, sustainable processes and products are healthy: they do not pose health risks to people or to the environment.

**Sustainable timber** See **Timber, sustainable**.

**Sycamore** This **hardwood** is a **sustainable timber** and is used for some furniture and domestic utensils. See the list of sustainable timber on p 155.

**Teak** Indonesia is the principal supplier of teak, a **tropical hardwood** that grows in the rainforests of Burma, Indonesia, and Thailand. It is used for floors, solid **wood** furniture, and veneers. Teak has become an endangered **timber** due to tropical deforestation and unsustainable management. Avoid products made from teak unless you are satisfied that the wood comes from managed plantations. See the list of **sustainable timber** on p. 155.

**Telephone** Various types of telephones can now be bought, but if you are considering changing yours, don't throw the old one away – return it to the manufacturer. The internal electrical components can be reused, and the metals and the **plastic** casing recycled.

**Television** See **TV**.

**Thermal storage** Commonly used in connection with **solar heating**, thermal storage is the storing of solar **energy** by means of **water** tanks and under-floor **concrete** slabs or rock beds.

**Thermometer** If you accidentally break a thermometer, take care when picking up the spilled **mercury**. This metal is quickly absorbed through the skin and any contact with mercury during pregnancy is thought to be harmful. Always use gloves to collect mercury, and take it to a pharmacy for disposal. Do not put it in the **trashbin** or down the drain.

**Thermoplastics** These soft plastics are flexible when heated and can **outgas**. Thermoplastics are used in various household products, and approximately 80 percent of **plastic** used today falls into this category. The most common thermoplastics include **PVC, polypropylene, polyethylene, polystyrene**, and **acrylic**. See **Plastic** and individual entries for types of thermoplastic.

**Thermosets** These **plastics** harden when heated and retain their shape. In general, thermosets do not give off vapors. In the home, however, exceptions to this rule include laminated **board** that contains **melamine formaldehyde**. Melamine is a plastic resin that is treated with **formaldehyde** to give a laminated finish to such board products as **plywood**. When new, formaldehyde vapor is given off. It can trigger allergies and is a suspected carcinogen. **Polyurethane, polyester**, and **silicone** are also thermosets. See **Plastic** and individual plastic entries.

**Thermoplastics**
**Thermosets**
**Thinner**
**Timber**

**Thinner** Common thinners for **paint** are **turpentine substitute** and **white spirit**. They are both, in fact, based on white spirit but the type used in turpentine substitute is of a lower grade. Thinners are **hydrocarbon solvents** that are toxic by inhalation, and can cause skin irritation. Long-term exposure to white spirit is associated with brain damage and has resulted in dermatitis. When using thinners, ensure that there is plenty of **ventilation**, and take care not to spill them on your skin. Thinners are also highly flammable substances so take precautions against fire. **Organic paint** suppliers offer a thinner based on citrus peel that contains no **petrochemicals** and dries more quickly than turpentine substitute or white spirit. You can also use pure **turpentine**, from some DIY stores, although it may trigger allergies in sensitive people.

**Timber** Forests are being destroyed worldwide at an alarming rate to satisfy global demands for timber. Every second, one acre of valuable rainforest disappears with disastrous environmental effects, including increased emissions of **carbon dioxide** (the major contributor to the **greenhouse effect**), soil erosion, and flooding. In the tropics, supplies of **tropical hardwoods** in such countries as Malaysia, Nigeria, and the Ivory Coast, are almost exhausted.

In the home, tropical hardwoods may be needed for some exterior applications but make every effort to see that they come from managed plantations, where felled trees are replaced on a **sustainable** basis. Hardwoods are rarely necessary for internal use but alternatives to tropical varieties include such indigenous timbers as **beech** and the softwood white cedar. A more sustainable alternative to hardwoods is use of fast-growing **softwoods** such as **pine** and **spruce** that are specifically grown in managed plantations for furniture and other domestic applications.

**Timber, sustainable**

Furniture made from **board** such as **MDF** with a decorative veneer is another alternative that is less damaging to the environment than using furniture made from solid tropical hardwood. MDF and **plywood** are usually manufactured from low-grade **softwoods** that are grown in a sustainable manner. Veneers, too, can mean a more efficient use of hardwoods: 50 veneered table tops can be made from the amount of **mahogany** required to make a single 1in thick solid-mahogany table. Some plywood, however, is made from tropical hardwood, so check with the store or timber merchant before buying. From the environmental standpoint, furniture with veneers made from temperate rather than tropical hardwood is always preferable. If you are chemically sensitive, board furniture may not be suitable because of the **formaldehyde** resin it contains. See **Timber, sustainable**.

**Timber, sustainable** Supplies of sustainably-produced **tropical hardwoods** are still relatively scarce. Indeed, some experts doubt if it is possible to manage tropical hardwoods on a truly sustainable basis. One alternative is to choose sawn timber and timber products that are made from both **hardwoods** and **softwoods** from the temperate regions of Europe and North America. For indoor use and furniture-making where decay is not an issue, such softwoods as **pine** or hardwoods as **beech**, are ideal. For external use, timber can be stained and treated with nontoxic **wood preservative** to increase its durability. For exterior application, consider using domestic moisture-resistant species such as white cedar. Another alternative to solid wood is to use such types of **board** as **chipboard**, **plywood**, or **medium density fiberboard**. Boards, however, contain

**formaldehyde**, an irritant chemical and a suspected carcinogen that is emitted as a vapor. A formaldehyde-free, cement-bonded chipboard may be available that is suitable for **flooring**.

In the UK, Friends of the Earth's Good Wood Seal of Approval is awarded to companies and traders who do not sell hardwoods or hardwood products unless they come from a sustainably managed source. Only choose timbers that have been sustainably managed.

The following table is a list of sustainable timbers, divided into hardwoods and softwoods, that are commonly available. The list is by no means exhaustive since timbers that are in limited supply have been excluded.

**Timber, sustainable (continued)**

| Hardwoods | Source |
| --- | --- |
| Ash, European | UK, Europe |
| Ash, White | North America |
| Aspen | North America, UK, Europe |
| Beech, American | North America |
| Birch, Yellow | North America |
| Maple, Rock | North America |
| Oak, American Red | North America |
| Oak, American White | North America |
| Oak, European | UK, Europe |
| Oak, Japanese | Japan |
| Poplar | UK, Europe |
| Walnut, Black | North America |

| Softwoods | Source |
| --- | --- |
| Cedar, White | North America |
| Fir, Douglas | North America, UK |
| Fir, Silver | UK, Europe |
| Hemlock, Western | North America |
| Larch, European | UK, Europe |
| Larch, Western | North America |
| Pine, Maritime | Europe |
| Pine, Pitch | North America |
| Pine, Southern | North America |
| Spruce, Canadian | North America |
| Spruce, Sitka | North America, UK |
| Spruce, Eastern | North America |
| Yew | UK |

**Timber treatments** For the home **timber**, lumber, or wood treatments fall into two categories: those you can buy from DIY stores and apply yourself, and those that require professional application. Into both categories fall **wood preservatives** for interior and exterior use, plus treatments to eradicate **dry and wet rot** and **woodworm killer**. These products contain **pesticides** and **fungicides** dissolved in **solvents**. For non-professional use, the active ingredients of such treatments include **acypetacs zinc**, **dichlofluanid** and **permethrin**. You may also come across obsolete products with small quantities of **pentachlorophenol (PCP)** and **tributyltin oxide (TBTO)**: both were formerly included in timber treatment products but have now been banned from products sold for DIY use. Professional timber treatment companies use products based on PCP, permethrin, TBTO, and some still use products containing **lindane**. Of these chemicals, lindane, PCP, and TBTO are extremely hazardous. There have been a number of cases of leukemia among workers exposed to lindane, and in homes and schools sprayed with this chemical symptoms ranging from nausea to poor concentration, and cases of aplastic anemia and epilepsy, have been reported. Lindane is banned in many countries and is classed as a carcinogen in the US. PCP is a nerve poison, causes a severe skin disease (chloracne), and damages the liver and heart. It also contains poisonous **dioxins**. TBTO is an irritant to skin and eyes, a suspected carcinogen, and may damage the immune system. According to the London Hazards Centre, people who have their homes sprayed with timber treatment chemicals will be exposed to the "largest pesticide dose of their lives".

**Timber treatments**

### Nonprofessional application

When considering DIY treatments for rot or woodworm, avoid products based on lindane and PCP. DIY products containing PCP and TBTO should no longer be available. Some manufacturers of wood preservatives have excluded these chemicals and use such alternatives as permethrin and acypetacs zinc. These substances are considered less hazardous, but should still be treated with caution since they are powerful skin and eye irritants, and the solvent vapors are harmful. Use these products only in well-ventilated areas; wear waterproof gloves, a mask, and protect your eyes. If you spill any of the product, wipe off splashes immediately and wash any exposed areas of skin thoroughly before eating. Guard against fire since the solvent in timber treatment products is highly flammable: some solvents can be ignited by a spark. Keep children and pets out of treated areas for at least 48 hours, and preferably for a week. Safer alternatives include a wood preservative based on **borax**. This comes in the form of a powder that can be dissolved in water and sprayed on timber. It does not emit vapor. Inorganic **boron compounds**, usually available as rods that are inserted in to predrilled holes in timber, are another alternative. Consider treating minor outbreaks of rot by eliminating the cause of moisture penetration, drying out the affected area with a dehumidifier, cutting out rotten lumber, and washing down the area with **bleach**. The most effective non-chemical method for controlling fungal rot is to eliminate sources of water penetration, protect timber with nontoxic borax preservative, and ensure that your home is kept warm, dry, and well ventilated. Treat exterior wood in vulnerable areas with nontoxic exterior preservative.

### Professional application

If you must have your home professionally treated to comply with building code regulations or mortgage requirements, first find a timber treatment company that does not use products based on lindane, PCP, or TBTO. Ensure that there is plenty of ventilation in areas to be treated and, while treatment is being carried out, move out, however inconvenient this may be. Do not return for at least 48 hours and preferably for one week. Do not sleep in treated bedrooms for at least seven nights, and keep all rooms well ventilated after application. Certain professional companies are prepared to use non-chemical methods to treat rot by cutting out lumber, eliminating the cause of moisture, and thereafter monitoring moisture levels. They may not, however, be prepared to guarantee work to the satisfaction of the agencies or institutions requiring it.

**Tires** Around 35 percent of scrap car tires could be recycled or remolded, but in the US this happens to only 9 percent of the 250 million tires discarded annually. Those remaining are dumped in landfills where they take up valuable space, do not decompose, and can lead to fires.▷

**Tires**

157

In Japan, 99 percent of tires are reused and in Germany 89 percent. Due to the low price of rubber and the absence of newer **recycling** technology for tires, recycling facilities are sometimes scarce. It is, therefore, difficult to be sure that your tires are recycled. What you can do, however, is to ensure that you use the most efficient type of tires and that you keep them properly inflated. Radial tires are the most economic and give you a six to eight percent saving on fuel. Underinflated car tires on the other hand, can waste fuel by up to five percent total.

**Titanium dioxide** This white **pigment** used in **paint** and most **toothpaste** as a whitener is a suspected animal carcinogen. The manufacture of titanium dioxide causes pollution in the form of acid effluents that are discharged into rivers and seas. Clear gel toothpaste does not contain titanium dioxide, neither do herbal toothpastes.

**Titanium dioxide**
**Tobacco smoke**
**Toilet**

**Tobacco smoke** More than 200 chemicals are present in tobacco smoke, and 40 of these are known carcinogens. Smoking pollutes indoor air, and higher concentrations are found in "sidestream" smoke than in the "mainstream" smoke that enters the smoker's lungs. US studies have shown that smoking in the home impairs the functioning of children's lungs. Never smoke when using products containing **solvents**. These substances are highly flammable, and chlorinated types will combine with tobacco smoke to form poisonous **phosgene** gas that is drawn directly into the lungs. Smoking in the presence of **radon** gas may also significantly increase the risk of cancer. If you smoke, set aside a room for this purpose and open windows. **House plants** will absorb pollutants from tobacco smoke; they work more efficiently if you group them together. Consider also investing in an **air cleaner** or an **ionizer** to help remove pollutants from smoke.

**Toilet** The toilet is the single biggest consumer of **water** in the home. A standard model can use up to 3.4 gallons per flush and can account for between 35 to 45 percent of total domestic water usage. A significant reduction of this considerable use of water can easily be achieved by placing two or three **bottles** filled with water inside the toilet tank to displace water. Weight them down with stones so that they cannot move and keep them clear of the moving parts. If you are buying a new toilet, choose the **dual flush** variety for greater water economy. This type of toilet, as the name implies, has two flushes and the shorter of the two can use as little as 1.3 gallons of water. Newer, efficient **low flush** toilets are also available that use only 1.8 gallons per flush. In the US, sales of low flush toilets rose from 30,000 in 1987 to 7.7 million in 1989. In Scandinavia and Germany, waterless compost toilets have been developed for sale in the States that efficiently process waste in the home. They are especially suitable for areas with limited or erratic water supplies, and they cut water consumption by about 50 percent.

**Toilet cleaner** Powdered toilet cleaners and **bleach** contain powerful chemicals that irritate the respiratory system and pollute waterways. Avoid bleach if you have a septic tank; it will kill the beneficial bacteria that break down your sewage. The chemical ingredients of acidic powders and bleach can also react together to form poisonous **chlorine** gas, so never use these two types of products at the same time. A safer way to clean your toilet without harming the environment is to pour undiluted white **vinegar** or sprinkle **bicarbonate of soda** into the bowl, leave overnight, then brush well in the morning. **Biodegradable** toilet cleaners based on vinegar are also available. These have a descaling and disinfecting action and are pleasantly scented with an **essential oil**.

Toilet cleaner
Toilet freshener block
Toilet paper

**Toilet freshener block** Many blocks contain **para-dichlorobenzene (PCDB)**, a toxic **insecticide** that persists in the environment and has been banned in many countries. Look for products that are PDCB-free, or add a few drops of a naturally disinfectant **essential oil**, such as pine, lavender, lemon, or eucalyptus to the water in the toilet bowl.

**Toilet paper** Around 500 million trees are cut down each year in the US to meet just the demand for **paper** and board. Choose recycled toilet paper, and make sure that bleached varieties have been treated with **oxygen bleach** rather than **chlorine bleach**. The chlorine-bleaching process, used to whiten pulp that is made into paper, produces toxic **dioxins** that seriously pollute the environment. Concern has also been expressed about possible dioxin contamination of the paper itself.

**Toiletries** When choosing toiletries, avoid **aerosols** that may contain environmentally-damaging propellant gases, and opt for **cruelty free** products if you object to **animal testing**. Many herbal toiletries are cruelty free and do not contain harsh **detergent** or synthetic fragrances. These will be gentler on your skin and hair. Avoid overpackaged products and consider buying from retailers that offer a refill service. See also individual entries for **Antiperspirant**, **Deodorant**, **Shampoo**, and **Toothpaste**.

**Toluene** A **solvent** commonly found in **adhesives** and **damp-proofing fluid**, toluene is a skin and eye irritant. It is harmful by inhalation and can result in damage to the central nervous system. Keep this product off your skin and only use in well-ventilated areas. Toluene is flammable, so keep it away from all sources of ignition. For safer alternatives, choose from the range of water-based, solvent-free adhesives available. Natural adhesives based on **organic** binders for **cork**, tile, **linoleum** and **carpeting** can be purchased from **organic paint** suppliers.

**Toothpaste** An ingredient of most brands of toothpaste is saccharin, a sugar substitute that is a known animal carcinogen. They also contain **titanium dioxide**, a **pigment** used for whitening the paste. This substance is a suspected animal carcinogen and an environmental pollutant. When effluent containing titanium dioxide from toothpaste manufacture is discharged, it acidifies rivers and seas. Choose instead clear gel toothpastes or herbal varieties: these do not contain titanium dioxide, and most herbal varieties are **cruelty free**. When cleaning your teeth, turn off the tap while brushing in order to save **water**.

**Toxic waste** See **Hazardous waste**.

**Trashbin** In the US, 154 million tonnes of domestic rubbish are generated every year. Before you throw anything into the trash, first consider whether it can be reused or recycled. A good idea is to have separate bins or containers in the **kitchen** (p. 16) or materials that can be recycled: one for **paper**, one for **metal**, one or more for **glass**, and one for waste food and vegetable matter to put on the compost heap. See also **Recycling**, **Waste**.

**Tributyltin oxide (TBTO)** This **fungicide** can be found in **timber treatments** for dry and wet rot, but for professional use only. TBTO has been banned from **wood preservatives** sold for DIY use. This corrosive and highly toxic chemical is a nerve poison and a powerful skin and eye irritant that causes burns and painful skin rashes. It is a suspected carcinogen and can damage the immune system. In the US, studies by the Environmental Protection Agency showed that it caused birth defects in laboratory animals. TBTO is also a serious environmental pollutant. Formerly employed as the active ingredient in anti-fouling **paint** for boats, it was banned because it interfered with and prevented reproduction in marine mammals.

Due to health risks, some manufacturers of timber-treatment products have eliminated TBTO from their products. If your home is being treated professionally, be sure that the products used by the treatment company do not contain TBTO. See **Timber treatments** for alternatives.

Tributyltin oxide (TBTO)

1,1,1-Trichloro-ethane (TCA)

**1,1,1-Trichloroethane (TCA)** An all-purpose **solvent** employed in a wide variety of products from **correction fluid** to **stain remover**. TCA is also known as **methylchloroform**. It may also be found in such **aerosol** products as suede and leather protector, and dry cleaning sprays, which do not contain **CFCs** and so are marketed as environmentally friendly. In fact, TCA is a serious atmospheric pollutant since it contains **chlorine** compounds that damage the **ozone** layer. Globally, it is estimated that 13 percent of the ozone-destroying chlorine in the upper atmosphere is attributable to TCA. Since this solvent has a shorter life than CFCs, UK Friends of the Earth consider it necessary to reduce levels over the short term. They are campaigning to establish a ban on TCA. From a health perspective, TCA can cause serious eye irritation; it is narcotic if deliberately inhaled, and long-term abuse can lead to psychological problems and damage to the nervous system and vital organs. In the US TCA is a suspected carcinogen, and it has been linked with miscarriages. Never smoke when using products containing TCA and keep it away from all sources of ignition: extremely poisonous **phosgene** gas can be produced if TCA is partially burned. Do not dispose of products containing TCA down the drain. Treat them as **hazardous waste** since the solvent persists once it's in the **water** supply. Avoid products containing this solvent. Choose water-based correction fluid and see **Stain remover** for a range of nontoxic alternatives.

**Trichloroethylene (Trike)** This **solvent** widely used in industry as a degreasing agent can also be found in products available from DIY stores, including **dry start** and **varnish remover**. In common with many solvents, trike is toxic by inhalation, producing symptoms of drowsiness and narcosis. Exposure to high concentrations can lead to cardiac arrest and damage to the spleen, liver, and kidneys. Trike causes cancer and birth defects in laboratory animals, and long-term exposure has been linked to liver damage and nervous disorders. Do not dispose of products containing this solvent down the drain as it persists in the **water** supply. According to US figures, one cup of trike can contaminate 3 million gallons of water. Only use products containing this solvent in well-ventilated conditions, do not inhale the vapor, and guard against fire as trichloroethylene is flammable. See **Varnish remover**.

**Trihalomethanes (THMs)** These substances are present in drinking **water** supplies in some regions. THMs – the most common is chloroform – are formed when water containing such **organic** matter as peat is treated with **chlorine**. THMs have been linked with cancer of the colon, rectum, and stomach. Contact your municipal water authority or a testing agency for an analysis of your water and for advice if you are worried about high levels of THMs. Using a **water filter** reduces chlorine compounds.

**Tropical hardwoods** Every second, one acre of irreplaceable tropical rainforest is being destroyed to satisfy the increasing demand for tropical hardwoods, to convert land to agriculture, and for cattle ranching. Commercial logging companies destroy or degrade an area of tropical forest equivalent in size to the UK annually. The heavy equipment needed to remove as little as one tree can seriously damage up to half an acre of forest, and for every cubic yard of **timber** extracted, the same quantity is wasted. Japan plays a major role in the tropical hardwood trade: Japanese companies own extensive areas of forest, especially in the Philippines and Malaysia, and there is major corporate investment in logging projects. Japan is the world's principal consumer of hardwoods: hardwood imports account for 50 percent of all the tropical timber imported by the industrialized world. Japan also exports tropical hardwoods to the West. Such hardwoods as **teak** are used extensively in Japanese homes for construction and panelling. They are also used for packing cases and disposable chopsticks. In the developed world, the UK, too, ranks as one of the biggest consumers of tropical hardwood, and 1987 Britain imported more than 2.3 million hardwood doors alone.

The scale of tropical deforestation has now reached critical proportions. According to some estimates, within 30 years there will be no rainforests left standing, except in the remotest regions of the world. Trees absorb **carbon dioxide ($CO_2$)**, the major contributor to the **greenhouse effect** and give out oxygen. But when trees are felled and forests burned, they not only cease to operate as a store for $CO_2$ but actually release it back into the atmosphere. $CO_2$ emissions from rainforests have increased by 75 percent in a decade. Deforestation, and particularly tropical deforestation, speeds up the greenhouse effect as well as robbing millions of indigenous peoples of their homes and their livelihoods. It also results in disruption of rainfall patterns, soil erosion, widespread flooding, and silting up of rivers. Rainforests are also valuable storehouses of raw materials and medicines. they contain more than half of the world's fast-disappearing species of plants and wildlife. **Sustainable** management – regulated felling and replanting – is practised in some forests but only 0.02 percent of tropical timber plantations fall into this category. There is, also, much controversy surrounding the concept of sustainable management of tropical hardwoods. Some authorities do not believe it is possible to carry out sustainable forest harvesting.

In the home, avoid tropical hardwoods unless you are satisfied that they come from managed plantations. If you need the durability of a hardwood, choose temperate hardwood, such as **beech** or **oak**. Hardwoods should not be necessary for such internal applications as furniture, internal doors, window frames, and molding. Consider using a fast-growing **softwood** such as **pine** or **spruce** instead. Such softwoods are grown specifically for furniture, joinery, and **paper** in a sustainable manner. You will also find some hardwoods that originate in countries with reforestation policies. See **Timber, sustainable**.

**Tropical hardwoods (continued)**

**Tumble dryer** This appliance consumes a great deal of **energy**. With an average consumption of around 2500 kWh per year, a tumble dryer is more expensive to run than a **washing machine**. Drying clothes out of doors is, of course, the best way of cutting energy consumption where possible or practical. To save energy, be sure that your wash has been well spun before drying, and, when choosing a washing machine, look for models with the best spinning efficiency. Avoid, too, over-drying your clothes: those that need ironing can be taken out slightly damp. Always make sure that the filter screen is clean. A filter with fluff deposits forces the the dryer to use up more power. If you are considering buying a tumble dryer, choose a model with a sensing device that automatically cuts off the power supply when the clothes are dry. **Gas** tumble dryers are a good option since gas is much more **energy efficient** and less polluting than electricity.

**Tungsten-halogen lamps** See **Halogen lamps**.

**Turpentine** Pure turpentine is a natural product distilled from a volatile oil, oleoresin It is present in the bark of certain varieties of **pine** tree. Turpentine was used to thin **paint** and clean brushes until the advent of synthetic **turpentine substitute**, or **white spirit**. Pure turpentine can also be mixed with **beeswax** to make **furniture polish**. Turpentine is harmful if inhaled, and can irritate the eyes, the skin, and the mucous membranes of sensitive people. If you are allergic to turpentine, use **thinner** based on citrus oils available from **organic paint** suppliers.

**Turpentine substitute** A **hydrocarbon solvent**, turpentine substitute is usually based on low-grade **white spirit** and used for cleaning brushes and thinning **paint**. It is toxic if inhaled and is also an irritant. Some varieties of turpentine substitute are suspected carcinogens. Keep this product away from all sources of ignition since it is highly flammable; do not inhale the vapor; and keep it off your skin. See **Thinner** for safer alternatives.

**TV** Color televisions consume an average of 150 kWh of electricity per year. Coal-fired power stations produce 36 million tons of **carbon dioxide ($CO_2$)** and 51,000 tons of **sulphur dioxide** per year to meet the electricity requirements for watching TV. **Energy efficient** TVs are available, but your current set may be using more electricity than you realize. Save **energy** and reduce emissions of $CO_2$, the main contributor to the **greenhouse effect**, from your existing model by making sure that your TV is switched off using the main switch on the appliance. "Switching off" the TV using some types of remote control means that your TV is on standby and continues to consume up to a quarter of the energy it uses when fully switched on. In the UK alone, Friends of the Earth have estimated that the wasted energy from TVs that have not been properly switched off costs $22 million per year and generates almost 221,000 additional tons of $CO_2$.

TVs also emit **electromagnetic radiation**, and this is considered harmful by some specialists. The **electromagnetic fields (EMFs)** are strongest near the set, so limit your viewing time and sit well back from your TV. Do not allow young children to sit too close up to the set. Low-radiation TVs have been developed in Sweden that also use less energy.

**TV
(continued)**

UFFI foam
Underlay
Upholstery
cleaner

**UFFI foam** This type of cavity-wall **insulation** foam contains **urea formaldehyde**, a powerful irritant and a suspected carcinogen. UFFI foam can **outgas**, releasing **formaldehyde** long after the initial installation, to cause indoor pollution. In Canada this type of insulation was banned due to health problems suffered by people with UFFI foam insulation in their homes. In the US, too, health problems resulted, in 1982, in a ban on UFFI foam, but the ban was subsequently overturned. Few buildings in the US have, however, been insulated with UFFI foam since 1982. Avoid UFFI foam and see **Insulation materials** for safer alternatives.

**Underlay** Synthetic rubber carpet backing is made from **petrochemicals** and the adhesive used to stick them to the carpet may contain harmful **solvents**. Synthetic backing is not durable and tends to disintegrate into powder after a few years, especially if any liquids are spilled on the carpet. Choose carpets with hardwearing natural hessian backing or a traditional felt underlay. Felt is made from recycled fabric.

**Upholstery cleaner** Shampoo and cleaner for upholstery, like **carpet cleaner**, is based on a **solvent**, usually **1,1,1-trichloroethane** or **perchloroethylene**, a solvent used in **dry cleaning**. Both these solvents give off toxic fumes and are serious environmental contaminants. 1,1,1-trichloroethane damages the **ozone** layer. See **Carpet cleaner**, **Stain remover** for alternatives.

**Upholstery filling** See **Polyurethane foam**.

**Urea formaldehyde** This substance is the active ingredient in synthetic **resins** that are used as binders in such types of **board** as **chipboard**, in **UFFI foam**, and in some hard **plastic**. It is made up of urea, synthesized from **ammonia** and **carbon dioxide**, and **formaldehyde**, a powerful irritant and suspected carcinogen. See individual entries for alternatives to products containing urea formaldehyde.

**Utile** This **tropical hardwood** is an endangered **timber**. Avoid products made from utile and see the list of **sustainable timber** on p. 155 for alternatives.

**Varnish** Before the advent of synthetics, varnish was based on **linseed oil**, and **lead** was used as a drying agent. Modern varnishes use such **petrochemical** derivatives as **polyurethane** and contain **solvents** including **toluene** and **xylene**. As the solvent evaporates, irritating fumes are given off, so only use polyurethane varnish in well-ventilated conditions. Varnishes now contain no added lead, but this does not mean that they are lead-free. They still contain a very small proportion. Natural varnishes are not as durable as synthetic varieties but they are safer and healthier. Consider first whether you really need a varnish: new and restored **wood** often needs no other finish than pure linseed oil or **beeswax**. Of the natural varnishes available choose **shellac**, a resin distilled from tropical trees that is an effective sealant. **Organic paint** suppliers also offer shellac varnishes that use linseed oil instead of solvents. Some varieties have an insect-repellent effect and others can be mixed with a **pigment** for added color.

**Varnish remover** Like **paint stripper**, varnish removers contain such harmful **solvents** as **dichloromethane (methylene chloride)**, **methanol**, and **trichloroethylene**. Some varieties may contain **caustic soda**. All these substances are harmful, especially the solvents; these are toxic by inhalation and if accidentally spilled on the skin. Varnish remover is also a serious **water** pollutant, so never pour it down the drain. See **Hazardous waste** for disposal. Use this product

167

only in well-ventilated conditions to help disperse the vapor, and guard against fire, as varnish remover is highly flammable. A safer alternative, available from DIY stores, does not contain dichloromethane or caustic soda and is largely **biodegradable**.

**VDT** See **Personal computer** and **Home office** (p. 176).

**VDT**
**Ventilation**

**Ventilation** With the advent of the modern, well-sealed building, the amount of ventilation in homes and offices is often greatly reduced. This can lead to the circulation of stale, polluted air. Also, people working in modern, sealed office blocks with quantities of electronic equipment and **air conditioning**, can suffer from a diverse variety of unpleasant symptoms, collectively known as **sick building syndrome**. Such health problems, however, are not exclusively confined to office workers; homes with sealed windows and air-conditioning systems can also harbor pollutants from appliances, fixtures, and furnishings. And these are not the only sources of indoor air pollution: common household products, from **adhesives** and **paint** to cleaning products, also give off potentially harmful vapors. Such pollutants, along with stale air, can build up and create health problems, ranging from headaches to sore throats and skin irritation. In the home, and especially the **home office** (p. 176), such electronic equipment as a **personal computer** or photocopier can deplete the beneficial negative ions in the air, and create static. Adequate ventilation is also necessary to prevent **condensation** and moisture, especially in the **bathroom** (p. 80) and **kitchen** (p. 16) – areas where moisture levels are high.

The simplest method of ventilating your home is to open windows. You can then increase air flow by opening windows on opposite walls thereby creating cross-ventilation. If this is not practicable, install **extractor fans**, particularly in the bathroom and kitchen. Consider a solar-powered model for greater economy. For added ventilation in the kitchen, install a **stove hood** as well as an extractor fan. Air-conditioning and mechanical ventilation systems are another alternative, depending on the climate, but use up a great deal of **energy**. They must be scrupulously maintained to avoid recirculation of pollutants and microorganisms from clogged filters or ducts. For individual rooms, consider portable filter units, or an **ionizer** to remove smoke and dust, and to reduce static. **House plants** also help to regulate indoor climate by maintaining humidity and absorbing pollutants. Most importantly, stop air pollution at its source by choosing natural and nontoxic materials for furnishing, cleaning, and maintaining your home.

**Vermiculite** This material is a type of **insulation** for lofts and attics and is also used for soundproofing. Vermiculite is one of a group of naturally occurring crystalline minerals that are light and water-absorbent. Unlike hazardous **UFFI foam** or **ozone**-damaging **polystyrene foam**, vermiculite is nontoxic and will not harm the environment. It comes in the form of chips that you pour between the rafters in your attic. Protective clothing is not necessary. See **Insulation materials** for other alternatives.

**Vinegar** This common kitchen ingredient made by fermenting beer, wine, or apples, is a natural source of **acetic acid**. The descaling, scouring, and disinfecting properties of acetic acid make vinegar an excellent, nontoxic household cleaner. Use distilled white vinegar in preference to the malt variety; the latter has added color that may stain. For an efficient **toilet cleaner**, pour undiluted white vinegar into the **toilet** bowl, leave it overnight and finish off with a brush in the morning. Vinegar also has descaling properties, so it will remove scale deposits at the same time. You can then add two or three drops of **essential oil** of pine or lavender for a pleasant scent. **Biodegradable** toilet cleaners based on concentrated acetic acid are also available in supermarkets and health food stores. Vinegar can also be used as a **descaler** for your **kettle**. Pour in equal quantities of water and white vinegar, boil the kettle, switch it off, and leave it for one or two hours. If the kettle is badly coated, leave the solution in overnight and finish off with a brush or nylon pot scourer. Vinegar also makes an excellent cleaner for **glass**, tiles, and other ceramic surfaces. Mix equal quantities of white vinegar and water and apply with a cloth. For easy application, especially when using the mixture as a **window cleaner**, fill a spray bottle, such as a plant spray, with the solution; spray on and wipe off with a soft cloth or kitchen towel. You can also use a 50/50 solution of vinegar and water to remove stains from tea and coffee pots, or from the insides of thermos bottles. Follow the method given for

**Vermiculite**
**Vinegar**

kettle descaling. Finally, vinegar makes a good **metal polish** for brass and copper. Polish with a mixture of hot white vinegar and salt, or with equal quantities of vinegar and **bicarbonate of soda**.

**Vinyl** This term refers to a group of **plastics**. The most common type of vinyl plastic found in the home is **polyvinyl chloride (PVC)** which is used to make **pipes, flooring**, sheeting for imitation leather upholstery, and as a **wallcovering**. Vinyl is also added to some types of **paint**. Vinyl prevents surfaces from "breathing", so it is not advisable to use vinyl wallcoverings, flooring, and paints in areas where moisture accumulates such as in the kitchen or bathroom. The vinyl covering simply traps any moisture, preventing evaporation and ventilation. This could eventually lead to problems with **moisture** and **mold**. Vinyls are thermoplastics, plastics that become soft when heated and release fumes. PVC is particularly hazardous since it can vaporize, releasing the raw material, **vinyl chloride monomer**, a known carcinogen. It is advisable, therefore, when laying PVC floor tiles to ensure thorough **ventilation** to disperse any fumes. A safer option is to avoid vinyl plastics whenever possible and see **Flooring, Wallcovering, Pipes**, and **Paint, organic** for alternatives.

**Vinyl**
**Vinyl chloride monomer**
**Volatile organic compounds (VOCs)**

**Vinyl chloride monomer** A chemical compound containing **chlorine**, vinyl chloride monomer is the raw material from which **PVC** is manufactured and is a known carcinogen. Vinyl chloride may still be used in some types of **clingfilm** food wrapping. However, in response to concern about the monomer migrating into fatty food, such as cheese and meat, warm food, or food wrapped for **microwave** cooking, many manufacturers have now removed PVC or PVC plasticizers from clingfilm.

**Volatile organic compounds (VOCs)** The principal characteristic of VOCs is that they contain volatile liquids and solids that are released as vapor at room temperature. Almost all these vapors are irritating, some are toxic. VOCs can be found in many household and DIY products including **paint, varnish, air freshener, polish**, and **stain remover**. See individual entries for alternatives.

**Wallcovering** There are a variety of wallcoverings to choose from including light or medium-weight **wallpaper**, heavy textured papers, **vinyl** wallcoverings, **cork** tiles, and such fabric wall coverings as hessian or **jute** cloths. Papering your walls will contribute a little toward preventing heat loss through external walls, but be sure that you have first sealed any cracks. Papers without waterproof finishes, and the fabric varieties without a **plastic** backing, will allow moisture to evaporate and enable the walls to "breathe". Vinyl wallcoverings, however, will trap in any moisture and prevent it from escaping, so avoid using them in the **bathroom** (p. 80) or **kitchen** (p. 16) where **moisture** or **mold** could be a problem. Vinyl also releases vapors at room temperature that may be irritating to sensitive people. If you are using lining paper with two or three coats of **paint** on top, water-based **emulsion paint** or **organic paint** is recommended. Using paint with added vinyl has a similar effect to vinyl wallpaper in terms of moisture evaporation, and the paint fumes may be hazardous while drying because of the **solvents** used.

**Wallpaper** See **Wallcovering**.

**Wallpaper paste** Most types of wallpaper paste are based on nontoxic **cellulose**, but they also commonly contain **fungicides**. Heavy-duty varieties may contain **polyvinyl acetate (PVA)**, a type of **adhesive**. Both fungicides and PVA may irritate the skin so wear gloves if your skin is particularly sensitive. Wallpaper paste, in a powdered form that does not contain synthetic fungicides or adhesives, can be obtained from **organic paint** suppliers, or you can make your own paste from flour and water.

**Walnut, Black** A temperate **hardwood**, walnut is a **sustainable timber** that is mainly used for veneers, high-quality furniture, and bowls. See also the list of sustainable timber on p. 155.

**Walnut, Black**
**Warfarin**
**Washing machine**

**Warfarin** A common anticoagulant **rat poison**, warfarin is also toxic to humans and pets if swallowed. It is also dangerous if inhaled. Wear gloves and treat this substance with great care, keeping it well away from children and pets. In some cases, rats have developed a resistance to warfarin, and even more powerful anticoagulants have been developed. If you suffer from hemophilia avoid all anticoagulant poisons: they work by preventing the blood from clotting so that rodents bleed to death. See **Rat and mouse poison** for alternative preventive measures.

**Washing machine** These appliances vary greatly in their consumption of **energy** and **laundry powder**; they also use on average between 26 and 52 gallons of **water** per wash. If you are choosing a new washing machine, make sure that it is as **energy efficient** as possible by choosing models with a lower wattage – around 1000 watts as opposed to 1800. The best new models use 40 percent less electricity and 55 percent less laundry powder than previous standard models. You can also make further savings on water consumption by choosing a washing machine that uses between 16 and 19 gallons per wash. Washing machines vary greatly in terms of length and speed of spin. If you are unable to hang your clothes outside to dry, a washing machine with a high spin speed will save on drying costs; the spinning period for washing machines with top spin speeds may be shorter.

With your existing machine, the most efficient way to save energy is to select a cycle with a lower washing temperature, and wait until you have enough wash for a full load. Many so-called half-load cycles use more than half the amount of water, powder, and electricity required for a full load, so are not economic.

**Washing soda** Washing soda has been a standard house-hold product for more than a century and it has an impressively wide range of applications in the home. The sodium carbonate crystals from which it is made are not known to be toxic, but always wear gloves when using washing soda to protect your hands. Use washing soda as a **stain remover** to remove blood, tea, and fruit juice from clothing. To clean stained tea and coffee pots, fill them with a solution of washing soda and leave for one to two hours. Soda crystals remove grease efficiently and are recommended for cleaning floors, walls, sinks, **stoves**, ovens, and drains. If the racks in your oven are particularly grimy, soak them in a washing soda solution and finish off with a scouring pad or wire wool. You can also use soda crystals to clean silver and to make **glass** sparkle. Added to **laundry powder**, they improve its cleaning power, act as a **water softener**, and make it go further.

Washing soda
Waste

**Waste** Each year, every person in the US throws away nearly two-thirds of a ton of rubbish. As a country, over 154 million tons of waste have to be disposed of annually, and 90 percent of it is dumped in landfill sites – craters in the ground that are filled with rubbish then covered over with clay and topsoil. Landfill sites are, however, becoming scarcer and most urban rubbish has to be expensively transported to ever-more distant locations, especially in such densely populated countries as the UK and Japan. London's waste is conveyed to over seven counties. In Tokyo, the situation is more serious, as landfill sites are expected to run out by 1992. America faces similar problems: a third of all available landfills are now full, and more than half the cities on the east coast have already run out of space to dump their waste. Existing landfills also harbor hidden dangers: an explosive gas composed of **methane** mixed with **carbon dioxide** is produced when rubbish decomposes. Another landfill hazard is leachate, a poisonous liquid produced by decomposing waste mixing with **water**. In many landfills the leachate cannot be pumped out and sinks below ground where it can find its way into the water table and go on to contaminate drinking water supplies. One method of disposal is to burn waste, while at the same time generating heat and power from it. In the Dutch city of Utrecht, burning household rubbish generates enough electricity for 100,000 people, and in Sheffield, UK, 80 percent of the city's rubbish is incinerated to supply heat and hot water to 4400 homes. Incineration, however, can itself produce toxic gases, heavy metals, and carcinogenic **dioxins** if the correct temperature controls are not adhered to, and if modern equipment has not been installed.

A first step toward solving the waste problem is to create less of it in the first place. An analysis by weight of the monthly rubbish thrown out by a typical family of four comprises the following: 25 percent waste food and organic matter; 30 percent **paper** and cardboard; 10 percent **glass**; 9 percent **plastic**; 10 percent metals; 4 percent textiles; and around 12 percent miscellaneous waste. It is also estimated that **packaging** materials alone account for 30 percent by weight of domestic waste. Buying less, avoiding over-packaged goods and reusing whatever we can is a positive step. The next stage is **recycling** as much of our waste as possible: glass, **aluminum** and steel, paper and cardboard, textiles, and some plastics can all be recycled to save both waste and **energy**. By the year 2000, the UK government would like to see 50 percent of all household waste recycled. Currently the figure is 10 percent, and in the US, 11 percent. Financial incentives for recycling would help establish markets for recycled products, while better facilities and more collection points for household waste are clearly necessary.

**Water-based paint**

### Steps you can take to reduce waste

- Choose durable products made from good-quality materials that are designed to last.
- Repair whatever you can, from shoes to vacuum cleaners, rather than throwing them away and buying new products.
- Avoid overpackaged goods, choose packaging materials that can be recycled, and take your own bags with you when you go shopping. Buying in bulk also saves on packaging and is cheaper.
- Buy goods in reusable, refillable, or returnable containers such as milk in **bottles**.
- Sort and separate your waste into containers ready for recycling, and recycle everything you can.

**Water-based paint** See **Emulsion paint**, **Paint**.

**Water** In the US, drinking water can contain three dozen or more chemicals that are associated with health problems, and in many areas of the country water supplies breach Safe Drinking Water Act (SDWA) standards. Indeed, many water authorities will be unable to comply with SDWA drinking water regulations for a number of years. The most prevalent water contaminants include **aluminum**, **lead**, **nitrates**, **pesticides**, **polycyclic aromatic hydrocarbons (PAHs)**, **solvents**, and **trihalomethanes**. In general, these pollutants are not removed by boiling water. In the US, over half of the total population relies on groundwater supplies for drinking water, and yet supplies in every state have suffered contamination from agricultural, industrial, and household chemicals. Water pollution in other countries, such as the UK also stems from environmental contamination, but can be exacerbated at the waterworks by the water authorities who treat it with aluminum or **chlorine**. Lead is dissolved in the water when it runs through lead supply pipes and, according to Friends of the Earth, accounts for a third of total lead intake. Children are particularly at risk from lead poisoning and it can damage the nervous system, kidneys, and the reproductive system. Nitrate and pesticide contamination occurs in regions where there is intensive agriculture, such as East Anglia, and high levels of nitrates have been linked to "blue-baby syndrome". Effluent from factories containing such toxic solvents as **trichloroethylene** has been discharged into rivers and leached into groundwater supplies due to inadequate disposal, while PAHs are released when the coal tar pitch, used until the mid-1970s to line water mains, breaks down. Many solvents are toxic and have been linked to birth defects, while some PAHs cause cancer in laboratory animals. Trihalomethanes are formed when water containing organic matter, for example peat, is chlorinated; studies have associated them with stomach and colon cancer.

Water

In some locations, water that is already polluted is treated with such potentially harmful substances as aluminum and chlorine. In the UK, aluminum sulphate is added to water to remove cloudiness and color, although excess levels of aluminum in the body are known to have been linked with Alzheimer's disease, or premature senility.

Pre-chlorination to disinfect drinking water supplies is also routinely administered by some authorities. this pro-

In recent years, the numbers of people working from home has shown a marked increase, and forecasts predict that by 1995 one-sixth of the workforce will be home-based. Home office equipment, furniture, and supplies, combined with poor seating, **lighting**, and inadequate **ventilation**, can often be a significant source of stress and health problems.

**VDT** There are various problems associated with working at VDTs – computer screens or monitors. Links between computer work by pregnant women and a higher, but not proven, risk of miscarriage have been put forward, and a correlation between VDT use and increased stress levels has been established. VDTs also emit low frequency **electromagnetic fields (EMFs)**. These fields are highest at the sides and back of the screen. These risks are not as great as that of repetitive strain injury (RSI). To reduce these risks, limit the amount of time at the screen and take frequent breaks. Choose a chair that supports your back and be sure that the keyboard is at a comfortable height. Fine mesh conductive screens help to reduce radiation and static.

**Electrical equipment** All electrical office equipment depletes the level of beneficial negative ions in the atmosphere. Install an **ionizer** to restore them; high levels of negative ions are associated with feelings of wellbeing. Computers, photo-

copiers and laser printers give off **ozone**. Photocopiers may emit **carbon monoxide** and are best kept out of the office in a separate, well-ventilated space. You can improve humidity and air quality with **house plants**. Plants filter indoor air and absorb pollutants; spider plants are particularly effective. Ensure also that your workspace is well ventilated.

**Desk and chair** Poor posture leads to back strain, RSI, and impaired concentration. Choose an adjustable chair that supports the small of the back, and a foot rest if it is too high. An office or typist's chair should have five base supports. Special posture chairs with angled seats and knee

1 Solid wood furniture
2 Full-spectrum bulb
3 Ionizer
4 Posture chair
5 Office supplies
6 Foot rest
7 Fine mesh conductive screen
8 Adjustable chair
9 Halogen lamp
10 Paper recycling basket
11 Cotton or wool rug
12 Wood floorboards
13 Photocopier in separate space
14 House plants
15 Window for ventilation and light

rests keep your spine comfortably straight.

**Lighting** Poor lighting and a lack of natural light will cause discomfort. Daylight is preferable to **artificial lighting** but avoid direct sunlight as the brightness and reflections can cause strain. Position your desk and screen at right-angles to the window, to avoid reflected light; an antiglare filter on your VDT will guard against eye strain. Avoid overhead **fluorescent light**: it may flicker and hum. Choose instead **halogen lamps** or use **full-spectrum** bulbs.

**Office furniture and carpeting**
Office furniture is frequently made from **board** products that emit **formaldehyde**, a suspected carcinogen. Synthetic carpeting will also have been treated with formaldehyde. Choose instead furniture made from solid **sustainable timber**. Choose such natural **flooring** materials as **wool** carpets, or **wood** floorboards with wool or **cotton** rugs.

**Office supplies** Many office supplies contain such harmful **solvents** as **1,1,1-trichloro-ethane**. This can cause dizziness, destroy ozone, and damage the eyes. Whenever possible, choose water-based varieties. Use office stationery made from recycled **paper**. Keep a bin in your workspace for **recycling** used paper, envelopes, and cardboard.

**Home office**

cess may produce chemical by-products known as chlorophenols, and also **dioxins**. These substances are then removed using charcoal filters. If the filters are not properly maintained, or if the chlorine combines with chemicals already in the water, excess levels of chlorophenols, which are suspected carcinogens, in the drinking water can result.

### Steps you can take to improve your water

**Water filters**

- Ask your municipal water authority to test your drinking water if, for example, you live in an area of intensive agriculture or if you suspect contamination. Water authorities are obliged by law to supply wholesome water and supplies should meet standards laid down by federal and state law. If you are not satisfied, inform your local Environmental Health Department.
- Replace any lead pipes in your home and make sure your municipal water authority has taken steps to replace any lead supply pipes.
- Buy a **water filter** or consider investing in an in-line or whole-house filtration system. Jug filters reduce the levels of most pollutants but currently only one type will reduce nitrates. Change your filter regularly.
- Try **bottled water** if you do not like the taste of your drinking water. Not all brands are purer than tap water; check the content of leading brands by consulting consumer surveys, such as those carried out by Consumers' Union, publisher of Consumer Reports.
- Support environmental groups that are campaigning for cleaner water.

**Water filters** According to some estimates, thousands of families a week are investing in water filters due to basic distrust of the purity of tap **water**, as well as dislike of the taste. The main purpose of water filters is to remove pollutants from drinking water. They also improve the taste, and reduce cloudiness and discoloration. Water filters, too, help to soften the water, preventing the buildup of limescale in the **kettle**. By law, filters must not add anything harmful to drinking water but there are no restrictions as to what they can take out. The choice of filters currently available is extensive, ranging from the relatively simple to increasingly complex systems, and there is a considerable variation in price. Put simply, water filters fall into three types: pour-through jugs, filters that fit on the tap, and in-line filters that fit under the sink. Whole-house line filter systems are also available to treat the entire home's water. Filters work using one of three methods: activated carbon, reverse osmosis, and distillation. For **nitrate** reduction, a separate unit is usually necessary.

### Activated carbon filters

In the home, the simplest and least expensive filtering system to install is the water-filtering jug. You simply pour water into a reservoir over the jug that houses a cartridge containing a mixture of activated carbon and ion exchange resins. The water then passes through the filtering cartridge and collects in the jug ready for use. Generally, the jug filters tested significantly reduced levels of **lead**, **trichloroethylene** (a **solvent**), **polycyclic aromatic hydrocarbons (PAHs)**, and **chlorine** from both hard and soft water. Most removed some **aluminum** from hard and soft water, and **iron** from hard water. Generally speaking, jug filters do not remove **nitrates** but some can reduce the amount. If you live in an agricultural region where nitrates are used extensively, ensure that you choose a nitrate-reducing filter or an in-line filter with a separate nitrate removal unit. With jugs, however, it is essential to replace your cartridge at the suggested intervals: the more water you filter, the more pollutants the cartridge absorbs and the lower its efficiency. A clogged filter can become a breeding ground for bacteria so ensure you install a new cartridge regularly. Bacteria also thrive in warm conditions so don't leave filtered water standing in a heated room for more than 24 hours. Store it in the **refrigerator** and wash the jug and reservoir attachment at weekly intervals. Activated carbon filters of the on-tap and in-line varieties are also widely available. The former fits on to the tap, and often contains added silver to prevent bacterial contamination. In-line activated carbon filters fit under the sink and the most effective types have a pre-sediment filter. One activated carbon filter-plus-silver, that was tested in Ohio, USA, was also claimed to remove significant quantities of **radon** from the water.

**Water filters (continued)**

### Reverse osmosis filters

This in-line filter fits under the sink, and usually comprises three canisters: the first pre-filters the water and removes solids; the second contains a membrane that lets through water but not pollutants; and the third contains a carbon filter to remove such **organic** chemicals as PAHs. Some reverse osmosis filters require a pump for the membrane that separates the water molecules from other molecules so, unlike activated carbon filters, you will need a power supply. Flow rates may also be slow, and, along with harmful chemicals, beneficial trace particles including calcium and **zinc** salts can also be removed. Reverse osmosis filters reduce levels of all contaminants, including **nitrates**, and can offer some protection against accidental pollution of the water supply by municipal water authorities.

### Distillation filters

Like the reverse osmosis systems, distillation filters are more complex and, initially, more expensive, than filter jugs. They do, however, achieve the highest level of water purity. They work by boiling tap water and then collecting the pure water that condenses from the rising steam. The pollutants are left in the base of the unit. Bacteria are killed and solids, metals, and trace particles are effectively removed. This type of filter also significantly reduces radon, but you will need to supplement it with a carbon filter; use it at the end of the distillation process to remove organic chemicals. Disadvantages are the very low flow rates of the distillation units, which can also make the water taste flat, and the extra cost of the carbon filter.

**Water softener** Hard **water** is a problem in a major percenage of homes, where it reduces the **energy efficiency** of domestic appliances including the electric **kettle** and the steam iron. Limescale deposits can also accumulate inside the water heater and radiators, resulting in substantially higher heating bills. Indications of hard water are blocked **shower** heads, and limescale in the kettle, in the **toilet** bowl, and around the bath taps. You also need to use more **laundry powder** and **dishwashing liquid** in hard water areas. Mechanical water softeners can be fitted in the **kitchen** (p. 16) if you live in such an area, but concern has been expressed at the high levels of sodium in the resulting water. A possible solution is to fit the softener to the hot water supply only. For drinking and cooking, however, all types of **water filter** will effectively soften the water and prevent limescale forming in kettles and steam

**Water softener**

irons. You can also cut down on the amount of washing powder and liquid you use by adding a commercial water softener to the water. Some, however, contain **phosphates** so choose a phosphate-free brand. See also **Descaler** for safe ways of removing limescale.

**Weatherproofing** Outdoor maintenance is essential if you are to avoid such serious and expensive problems as **moisture** and rot. Each year, and after stormy weather with high winds, inspect the roof and replace any damaged or missing shingles, tiles, or slates to prevent water penetration. Be certain, too, that there is adequate **ventilation** in the attic to prevent **condensation**, and that holes in vents under the eaves have not been blocked by **insulation**. Covering flat roofs with **bitumen** or bituminous **paint** will make them waterproof, but bitumen is a skin irritant, so wear gloves when using it. Damaged gutters and flashings must be repaired, and cracks in stucco or parging covering the house must be filled. **Pipes** and gutters can become blocked with leaves and debris and lead to overflows, while old **iron** downspouts can rust through. Clear out gutters and repair any defective downspouts. Check also that wooden window frames have not deteriorated and that the paint is in good condition. Exterior paints, primers, and **wood preservative** commonly contain irritant and harmful substances including **dichloromethane**, **methanol**, and **dichlofluanid**. Keep products containing these substances off your skin, and do not inhale the vapors. See **Paint, organic**, **Primer**, and **Wood preservative**.

Weatherproofing
Weatherstripping

**Weatherstripping** Eliminating drafts that flow around doors, between floor and baseboards, and through **windows** saves **energy** and cuts fuel bills. Around one-sixth of your heat escapes via cracks and gaps. Weatherstripping could reduce this by a third and is inexpensive to use. Fit weatherstripping around windows, below doors, and seal gaps between floorboards and walls with **wood** moldings, or even felt, if you do not have fitted carpets. In rooms with a **gas** heater, or an open fire, be sure that the heater is vented to the outside, and that the chimney flue is not blocked. These measures, together with efficient **ventilation**, will prevent the build up of harmful gases. See also **Insulation** and **Ventilation**.

**White spirit** Used for thinning oil-based **paint** and for cleaning brushes, white spirit is a volatile **solvent**. Some people may be sensitive to the vapor given off, and exposure over a period of time has resulted in central nervous system damage. Prolonged exposure can also result in severe skin irritations. Do not remove paint from your hands with white spirit, especially if you have sensitive skin. If you are using this substance, protect your skin and do not inhale the vapors. White spirit is also highly flammable so guard against fire. A safer, alternative, **paint thinner** and brush cleaner based on plant oils can be obtained from **organic paint** suppliers. You can also use pure **turpentine**, but some people may be sensitive to the vapor, which is a skin and an eye irritant.

**Whitewash** See **Limewash**.

**Windows** To maximize light, especially important during the winter months, ensure that windows are always clean, and that curtains draw back fully from the window area. If you plan to install new windows, raising the height is a more effective method of increasing daylight than widening them. Skylight and rooflights will also admit maximum daylight. To prevent heat escaping from windows, make sure that any cracks are sealed. In winter, an inexpensive form of **insulation** is to **weatherstrip** windows and to hang heavy curtains, always drawing them at dusk. **Double glazing** is expensive to install and the initial outlay will take several years to recoup. As an **energy-saving** device, however, double glazing is worth considering if you are having new windows installed anyway. Make sure that you have enough **ventilation** by opening windows, especially when using the **bathroom** (p. 80) and **kitchen** (p. 16) – places where moisture can build up. Always check that exterior woodwork around windows is in good condition and that the paint has not deteriorated. Water penetration through window frames and sills can lead to serious rot outbreaks. **Organic paint** suppliers recommend treating windows with their stains as they bond to the wood more effectively than synthetic finishes, and allow it to "breathe".

**Window cleaner** Commonly contains **ammonia**, an irritant to the eyes and the respiratory tract. **Aerosol** varieties of window cleaner are especially hazardous as the fine mist is easily inhaled. Some window and glass cleaners may also contain a **formaldehyde** preservative. An effective, nontoxic alternative cleaner for windows and **glass** surfaces in the home is white **vinegar**. Mix equal parts of white vinegar and water in a spray bottle, such as the type used for plants. Spray on the solution and polish off with a soft cloth, kitchen towel, or newspapers. If repeated applications of commercial cleaners have left a waxy coating on the glass, first clean the windows with **washing soda** or isopropyl alcohol, then use the vinegar-and-water solution. You can also buy nontoxic glass and ceramic cleaners based on **acetic acid** that are suitable for **windows**. These are free from **phosphates** and formaldehyde.

**Wood**
**Wood preservative**

**Wood** When choosing lumber or sawn wood for your home, or wooden furniture, avoid **tropical hardwoods** unless they come from a **sustainable** source. Tropical hardwoods come mainly from rainforest areas and it is estimated that the rate of rainforest clearance is now one acre per second. This large-scale destruction, due mainly to logging and ranching, is resulting in floods and droughts; the disruption of global weather patterns; the release of large quantities of the main greenhouse gas, **carbon dioxide**; the homelessness of indigenous peoples; and the extinction of many of the planet's species. Temperate **hardwoods** and **softwoods** are good alternatives. For further information, see the list of **sustainable timber** on p. 155.

**Wood preservative** Preservatives for use in the home contain substances similar to the harmful chemicals found in **timber treatments** for rot. Common ingredients of wood preservatives for nonprofessional use that are available in DIY stores include **dichlofluanid, permethrin,** and various **solvents**. Products containing highly toxic **pentachlorophenol** and **tributyltin oxide** have now been banned for DIY use and should not be available for sale . Dichlofluanid is a skin and eye irritant, and there is some evidence that it causes genetic damage to laboratory animals. Permethrin is considered safe for places where bats roost, but in humans it is a skin and eye irritant, and it has been linked with damage to the nervous system. According to the US Food and Drug Administration, permethrin is a suspected carcinogen. Never pour unused wood preservative down the drain as it is a serious **water** pollutant and will harm fish. See **Hazardous waste** for disposal. The solvent vapors from preservatives are also highly irritating and the solvent content makes these products flammable. When using wood preservatives, wear a mask and protect your eyes and skin. Make sure also there is plenty of ventilation, and take precautions against fire. Products that contain **acypetacs zinc** are considered less toxic than those based on dichlofluanid or permethrin, but a safer alternative is to treat wood, both interior and exterior, with preservatives obtainable from **organic paint** suppliers. Based on **borax** and resin oils, and free from solvents, these nontoxic preservatives come in powder form that can be dissolved in water and sprayed on wood. They do not emit vapors so will not pollute indoor air.

**Woodworm killer**
**Wool**

**Woodworm killer** Until it was banned in 1989, woodworm killer commonly contained dieldrin, a toxic **insecticide**. The active ingredient of woodworm killer currently on sale is usually **permethrin** in a **solvent** base. Permethrin is less hazardous than dieldrin: in the US, however, it is a suspected carcinogen. The solvent vapors that evaporate from woodworm killer are also irritating and they can cause skin problems. When using woodworm killer, wear a mask and protect your skin and eyes. Make sure also that there is plenty of ventilation and guard against fire. Woodworm thrives on **moisture** and high levels of humidity. If your house has **central heating**, is well-ventilated, and free from moisture, woodworm infestations are unlikely. For woodworm in furniture, heat treatment is a safe alternative, but it is not appropriate for furniture with joints that have been glued together. A preventative measure you can take to stop woodworm laying eggs is to impregnate the wood with a **borax** solution, or treat wood surfaces with a nontoxic, natural **varnish**, or with a **beeswax** polish. Woodworm eggs cannot penetrate painted or polished surfaces.

**Wool** Pure wool has excellent thermal qualities and is also naturally **fire retardant** due to its water and protein content. The manufacturing process for wool products uses few chemicals, except for the bleaching and removal of grease. Before sale, however, most woolen **fabrics**, clothing, and **carpeting** are mothproofed. To reduce any **pesticide** residues, steam-clean carpets before use. You can also obtain rugs and clothing made from unbleached and untreated wool, as well as from vegetable-dyed wool. Make a point to look for Indian *dhurries* and Turkish rugs from ethical traders. These are handwoven and usually colored with vegetable dyes. Chemical-free wool **futons**, mattresses, and fleece underblankets are also available.

**Wool
(continued)**

**Xylene** Xylene is a **solvent** belonging to the group of chemicals known as **hydrocarbons**; it is commonly found in metal **primer**, and in **dry start** for cars. In high concentrations, the vapors given off by xylene cause drowsiness, and prolonged exposure can produce dizziness, irritability, and anxiety. Xylene is also a skin irritant. When using products containing xylene, do not breathe in the vapor and make sure that there is plenty of ventilation. Keep xylene off your skin and take precautions against fire as it is highly flammable. See **Primer** for safer alternatives.

**Yew** A strong, durable **softwood** that is native to the UK, yew is a **sustainable timber**. It is used for furniture and interior joinery. For other sustainable timbers see the list on p. 155.

**Zeolites** Zeolites are naturally-occurring crystals of sodium aluminium silicate that are formed in a similar fashion to pumice stone. They are commonly used in **laundry powder** as a substitute for **phosphates**, due to their water-softening properties. Unlike phosphates, zeolites do not cause **water** pollution and are not known to harm the environment in any other way.

**Zinc** This blue-white metal is used in galvanizing and in a number of alloys. Zinc flashings – seals used to waterproof joints on the roof – are found on older buildings.

Zinc can be damaged in areas where there is **acid rain**, and **lead** is preferred as it is more durable. Used in this way, however, zinc is unlikely to pose any health hazards.

**Zinc naphthenate** Derived from the naphthenic acids that occur in **petroleum**, zinc naphthenate is used as a **fungicide** and may be found in some **wood preservative**. There is little information about this substance but it is considered safe to use in attics where bats roost. Due to shortages and, therefore, the availability of only lower-quality naphthenic acids with inferior fungicidal properties, one manufacturer of wood preservatives has synthesized a superior compound from zinc salts called **acypetacs zinc**. This substance is used as a substitute for zinc naphthenate, **pentachlorophenol** and **tributyltin oxide** in wood preservatives and other **timber treatments**.

**Zinc phosphate** Commonly found in **primer** for metal and in antirust treatments, zinc phosphate is not known to be toxic. It is preferable to the **lead** that was formerly used in such primers.

# Organizations

## General

Consumers' Union
256 Washington St.
Mt. Vernon, NY 10553

## Environmental

Alaska Wildlife Alliance
P.O. Box 202022
Anchorage, AK 99520

Center for Marine
Conservation
1725 DeSales St. NW
Washington, DC 20036

Citizen's Clearinghouse for
Hazardous Waste
P.O. Box 926
Arlington, VA 22216

Defenders of Wildlife
1244 19th St. NW
Washington, DC 20077

Director, Office of Program
Development
U.S. Environmental Protection
Agency
401 M St. SW
Washington, DC 20460
Tel (202) 475-7751

Earth First!
P.O.Box 235
Ely, NV 89301

Environmental Action
1525 New Hampshire NW
Washington, DC 20036

Environmental Defense Fund
257 Park Ave. South
New York, NY 10010

Friends of the Earth
530 7th Street SE
Washington, DC 20003

Greenhouse Crisis Foundation
1130 17th St. NW, Suite 630
Washington, DC 20036

Greenpeace
1436 U St. NW
Washington, DC 20009

National Audubon Society
950 Third Avenue
New York, NY 10022

National Coalition Against
Misuse of Pesticides
530 7th St. SE
Washington, DC 20003

National Wildlife Federation
8925 Leesburg Pike
Vienna, VA 22184

Natural Resources Defense
Council
40 West 20th St.
New York, NY 10011

Rainforest Action Network
300 Broadway, Suite 28
San Francisco, CA 94133

Sierra Club
730 Polk St.
San Francisco, CA 94109

The Nature Conservancy
1815 North Lynn St.
Arlington, VA 22209

The Wilderness Society
1400 I St. NW
Washington, DC 20005

Worldwatch Institute
1776 Massachusetts Ave. NW
Washington, DC 20036

World Wildlife Fund
1250 24th St. NW
Washington, DC 20037

## Anti-cruelty

Animal Legal Defense Fund
1363 Lincoln St., No. 7
San Rafael, CA 94901

Doris Day Animal League
Suite 200
111 Massachusetts Ave. NW
Washington, DC 20001

National Anti-Vivisection
Society
53 West Jackson Blvd.
Chicago, IL 60604

The American Anti-Vivisection
Society
Suite 204 Noble Plaza
801 Old York Rd.
Jenkintown, PA 19046

The American Society for the
Prevention of Cruelty to
Animals
411 East 92nd St.
New York, NY 10128

The Animal Protection
Institute of America
6130 Freeport Blvd.
Sacramento, CA 95822

The Humane Society of the
United States
2100 L St. NW
Washington, DC 20037

## Building

Housing & Urban
Development User
P.O. Box 6091
Rockville, MD 20850

Housing Resource Center
1820 West 48th St.
Cleveland, OH 44102

International Institute for
Baubiologie & Ecology
P.O. Box 387
Clearwater, FL 34615

National Association of Home
Builders
National Research Center
400 Prince Georges Blvd.
Upper Marlboro, MD 20772

National Association of
Plumbing-Heating-Cooling
Contractors
180 South Washington St.
Falls Church, VA 22046

## Energy Efficiency

CAREIRS
P.O. Box 8900
Silver Spring, MD 20907

Director, Office of Building &
Community Systems
U.S. Department of Energy
1000 Independence Ave. SW
Washington, DC 20585

Energy Efficient Building
Association
Technology Center
University of Southern Maine
Gorham, ME 04038

Energy Rated Homes Program
100 Main St.
Little Rock, AR 72201

Minnesota Energy
Information Center
150 East Kellog Blvd.
St. Paul, MN 55101

National Appropriate
Technology Assistance Service
P.O. Box 2525
Butte, MT 59702

Rocky Mountain Institute
1739 Snowmass Creek Road
Snowmass, CO 81654

Southface Energy Institute
P.O. Box 5506
Atlanta, GA 30307

## Health and Safety

American Lung Association
1740 Broadway
New York, NY 10019

Electric Power Research
Institute
Energy Management Division
Residential
3412 Hillview Ave.
Palo Alto, CA 94304

Environmental Health
Network
P.O. Box 575
Corte Madera, CA 94925

Environmental Health Watch
4115 Bridge Ave.
Cleveland, OH 44113

Human Ecology Action
League, Inc.
P.O. Box 66637
Chicago, IL 60666

National Institute for
Occupational Safety & Health
4676 Columbia Parkway
Cincinnati, OH 45226

Chemical Hazards Program
U.S. Consumer Products
Safety Commision
5401 Westbard Ave.
Room 419
Bethesda, MD 20207

## Organic Gardening

California Certified Organic
Farmers
Box 8136
Santa Cruz, CA 95061

Ecology Action/Common
Ground
5798 Ridgewood Rd.
Willits, CA 95490

National Gardening
Association
180 Flynn Avenue
Burlington, VT 05401

Natural Organic Farmers
Association
140 Chestnut St.
West Hatfield, MA 01088

Regenerative Agriculture
Association
222 Main St.
Emmaus, PA 18049

## Vehicles

American Solar Car
Association
P.O. Box 158
Waldoboro, ME 04572

International Human Powered
Vehicle Association
P.O. Box 51255
Indianapolis, IN 46251

Northeast Solar Energy
Association
P.O. Box 541
Brattleboro, VT 05301

## Waste and Recycling

Aluminum Recycling
Association
1000 16th St. NW
Washington, DC 20036

American Paper Institute
Recycling Committee
260 Madison Ave.
New York, NY 10016

American Petroleum Institute
1220 L St. NW
Washington, DC 20005

Glass Packaging Institute
1801 K St. NW
Washington, DC 20006

National Association of
Solvent Recyclers
1333 New Hampshire Ave
NW, Suite 1100
Washington, DC 20036

National Recycling Coalition
P.O. Box 80729
Lincoln, NE 68501

Rubber Recyclers Association
2233 Tyrone St.
Akron, OH 44312

Society of the Plastics Industry
1275 K St. NW Suite 400
Washington, DC 20005

Steel Can Recycling
Association
Two Gateway Center
Suite 720
Pittsburgh, PA 15222

The Aluminum Association
900 19th St. NW
Washington, DC 20006

**Resources**

189

# Suppliers

## Mail Order Catalog

A Brighter Way
P.O. Box 14486
Austin, TX 78760

Atlantic Solar Products
P.O. Box 70060
Baltimore, MD 21237

Baubiologie Hardware
207 Sixteenth St. Unit B
Pacific Grove, CA 93950

Bio-Sun Systems
Box 134-A RD 2
Millerton, PA 16936

Earth Care Paper
P.O. Box 14140
Madison, WI 53714

Real Goods Trading
Corporation
966 Mazzoni St.
Ukiah, CA 95482

Self-Care Catalog
349 Healdsburg Ave.
Healdsburg, CA 95448

Seventh Generation Products
Box 1672
Colchester, VT 05446

Solar Components
Corporation
121 Valley St.
Manchester, NH 03103

The Allergy Store
P.O. Box 2555
Sebastopol, CA 95473

The Sun Electric Co.
P.O. Box 1499
Hamilton, MT 59840

The Vermont Country Store
P.O. Box 3000
Manchester Center
VT 05255

Windpower
Rt. 1
Holton, KS 66436

Yellow Jacket Solar
Box 253
Yellow Jacket, CO 81335

## Air Systems and Ionizers

Airguard Industries, Inc.
P.O. Box 32578
Louisville, KY 40232

AllerMed
31 Steel Rd.
Wylie, TX 75098

Control Resource Inc.
670 Mariner Dr.
Michigan City, IN 46360

## Beds and Bedding

Dona Designs
825 Northlake Dr.
Richardson, TX 75080

Eugene Trading Co.
339 East 11th
Eugene, OR 97401

Garnet Hill
P.O. Box 262
Franconia, NH 03580

Northwest Futon
P.O. Box 14952
Portland, OR 97214

The Company Store
500 Company Store Rd.
La Crosse, WI 56401

The Cotton Place
P.O. Box 59721
Dallas, TX 75229

The Futon Shop
491 Broadway
New York, NY 10012

## Cosmetics, Toiletries and Healthcare

InterNatural
P.O. Box 580
South Sutton, NH 03273

Simplers Botanical Co.
P.O. Box 39
Forestville, CA 95436

The Body Shop Inc.
45 Horsehill Rd.
Cedar Knolls, NJ 07927

Tom's Natural Products
Kennebunk, ME 04043

Weleda Pharmacy
841 South Main St.
Spring Valley, NY 10977

## Electromagnetic Pollution Protection

Baubiologie Hardware
See under Mail Order

Environmental Testing and
Technology
P.O. Box 369
Encinitas, CA 92024

## Energy Efficient Appliances

Kachelofen Institute
P.O. Box 3339
Ashland, OR 97520

Low Energy Systems
2916 South Fox St.
Englewood, CO 80110

Thermal Energy Storage
Systems
RR 1 Box 3 Beanville Rd.
Randolph, VT 05060

Vermont Castings
Randolph, VT 05060

## Flooring

Carousel Carpet Mills
1 Carousel Lane
Ukiah, CA 95482

Farbo North America
P.O. Box 32155
Richmond, VA 23294

SelfHelp Crafts
704 Main St.
Akron, PA 17501

## Furniture

Oakworks Inc.
427 South Main St.
Shrewsbury, PA 17361

Shaker Workshops
P.O. Box 1028
Concord, MA 01742

Willsboro Wood Products
Box 336
Willsboro, NY 12996

## Household Cleaning Products

Seventh Generation; Real
Goods Trading Corp.;
Self Care; Baubiologie
Hardware
See under Mail Order

## Lighting

Duro-Test Corp.
2321 Kennedy Blvd.
North Bergen, NJ 07047

Environmental Systems Inc.
1140 Dillerville Rd.
Lancaster, PA 17601

Kyocera International Inc.
8611 Balboa Ave.
San Diego, CA 92123

Network Marketing Healthy
Lights
25 West Fairview Ave.
Dover, NJ 07801

## Paints and Finishes

AFM Enterprise Inc.
1140 Stacy Court
Riverside, CA 92507

Miller Paint Co.
317 SE Grand Ave.
Portland, OR 97214

Murco Wall Products
300 NE 21st St.
Fort Worth, TX 76106

Nigra Enterprises
5699 Kanan Rd.
Agoura, CA 91301

Pace Chemical Industries
Inc.
779 South La Grange Ave.
Newbury Park, CA 91320

Weatherall Northwest
295 Lost Horse Rd.
Hamilton, MT 59840

William Zinsser and Co.
39 Belmont Dr.
Somerset, NJ 08875

## Water Filters and Purifiers

Aquathin Corp.
2800 West Cypress Creek
Ft. Lauderdale, FL 33309

Mid America Water Purity
12839 Chillicothe Rd.
Chesterland, OH 44026

Pure Water Place, Inc.
P.O. Box 6715
Longmont, CO 80501

Simco Associates
1426 Martin Dr.
Colorado Springs
CO 80915

## Testing Services

### Carbon Monoxide

Quantum Group Inc.
11211 Sorrento Valley Rd.,
No. D
San Diego, CA 92121

### Formaldehyde

Applied Technical Services
Inc.
1190 Atlanta Industrial Dr.
Marietta, GA 30066

Air Quality Research Inc.
901 Grayson St.
Berkeley, CA 94710

## Lead

Applied Technical Services
See above

Urbco Products Co.
31 Haynes St.
Worchester, MA 01603

## Radon

Air Chek
P.O. Box 2000
Arden, NC 28704

Glenwood Laboratories
3 Science Rd.
Glenwood, IL 60425

Radon Testing Corporation
of America
12 West Main St.
Elmsford, NY 10523

The Radon Project
P.O. Box 90069
Pittsburgh, PA 15224

## Water

National Testing Labs
6151 Wilson Mills Rd
Cleveland, OH 44143

Water Test Corp.
33 South Commercial St.
Manchester, NH 03108

## Acknowledgements

Gaia books would like to
thank the following for their
help in producing this book:
Chemical consultant Hugh
MacGrillen, US consultant
Richard Freudenberger;
David Pearson and Hartwin
Busch; Philip Parker and
Isabelle Gore for editorial
assistance; Susan Walby and
Alison Jones for production;
Sara Mathews for design
co-ordination; Phil Gamble
for design assistance;
Samantha Nunn and
Martha Zenfell, and very
special thanks go to
Lesley Gilbert for text
management.

Resources